The Non-Designer's Presentation Book

principles
for
effective
presentation
design

P9-DDI-970

Robin Williams

Peachpit Press
Berkeley
California

The Non-Designer's Presentation Book
ROBIN WILLIAMS

©2010 by Robin Williams

Peachpit Press
1249 Eighth Street
Berkeley, California 94710
510.524.2178   voice
510.524.2221   fax

Editor:	Nikki Echler McDonald
Proofer:	Patricia Pane
Cover design and production:	John Tollett
Interior design:	Robin Williams
Production:	Robin Williams
Index:	Robin Williams

Peachpit Press is a division of Pearson Education.

Find us on the web at www.peachpit.com.

To report errors, please send a note to errata@peachpit.com.

ISBN 13: 978-0-321-65621-6

ISBN 10: 0-321-65621-0

10 9 8 7 6 5 4 3 2

Printed and bound in the United States of America

This book is dedicated to
every single person who
has bought a copy of
The Non-Designer's Design Book,
especially those of you who
have written to tell me
how much it meant to you.
Thank you so much!
I wrote this one for you.

Contents

BEFORE YOU DESIGN

OPTIMIZE THE CONTENT

4 Relevance   45

5 Animation   55

6 Plot   65

Design is about learning to see
mindfully.

DESIGN THE SLIDES

The text is data;
the images are emotion.

BEYOND THE PRINCIPLES

Foreword from John Tollett

Robin has given millions of successful presentations in the past twenty years (hundreds, actually, but millions has a nice ring to it). She says she's learned from each one and keeps getting better, and happily, so did the software. Today there are many, many presentation books on the shelves, and she's studied just about all of them. From my point of view, most of those books are, well, ponderous, pretentious, and confusing.

One of Robin's goals was to write the book she wishes she'd had twenty years ago, when she started giving presentations to schools, conferences, organizations, and workshops. A book that cuts to the chase and tells you what you need to know right now for that presentation that's due this week. In this book, you'll find great design tips and great software tips. That's because Robin's obsessed with design and typographic excellence. And it shows in the more than 60 books she's written, designed, and produced (most of them award-winners and best-sellers).

There are three things you must know and accept before attempting to create a good digital presentation:

It takes time. You need to gather and organize your content, create effective slides in your preferred software, and rehearse. There's no way around this. Of course, you can create a functional and perhaps passable digital presentation in a short amount of time, but to create a good or great one, you need to invest the time.

You must learn your software. You cannot create a good presentation unless you know how to use the software. Read the manual. Read the help files. Take a class. PowerPoint likes to take over your formatting, so if you want control over your slides (which of course you do), you must learn how to circumvent its automatic features and take charge.

Everyone expects more these days. Thanks to television, DVDs, keynote speeches and conferences broadcast on the Internet, and even professional presenters on tour, your audience has raised the bar for slide presentations. The advent of communication technology has put you in competition with the best presenters in the world. You can still get away with bad design and schlocky presentations, but now everyone knows just how bad it really is.

Since you're holding this book, you are obviously interested in learning how to design visually interesting and professional-looking slides. You are so lucky you chose this book! I'll bet you'll actually read this one. And it'll make a difference.

Robin has outdone herself, creating a book that's destined to be as popular as her earlier best-seller, *The Non-Designer's Design Book,* which has influenced non-designers, professional designers, and yes, even other design authors, the world over. —*jt*

So YOU have to give A PRESENTATION

BEFORE YOU DESIGN

The credibility of a speaker depends not merely on the strength of her prepared arguments, but on the audience's perceptions of the speaker. This was the reality taught by the ancient Greeks and Romans and renewed again during the European Renaissance. We're coming back to this way of thinking today.

Presentations are no longer staged, one-way affairs. People are often twittering, posting, texting, and chatting with others around the world as they listen to you. If you step onto that stage with a flimsy story or a visually feeble presentation, the world will know immediately. Gone are the days when you could get away with being dull. Step up to the challenge.

You may be an incredible dullard in real
life, putting people to sleep right and
left, but at that podium, you're a star.
You're an entertainer, an educator,
put on a happy face and kick ass . . .
or get off that stage.

J.H. Lehr
"Let there be stoning!" *Ground Water*, v. 23, no. 2, p. 164

Where to begin?

Although this book focuses on the *design* of your computer presentation, the primary thing to remember is that your presentation is not merely the computer file—it's *you*. YOU give the presentation, and your computer file simply helps you in that task.

You can, of course, create a stand-alone presentation to post on a web site, and the principles in this book still apply, except that everything you might talk about would have to be on the slides or, preferably, in the accompanying speaker notes.

But the focus of this book is on designing digital presentations that supplement your dynamic self, presentations that augment your *talk,* that contribute to persuading or informing your audience. All the graphics and animation and audio and video that go into your project are held together and presented by YOU. *You* are the star.

What's a presentation?

The very nature of a presentation, as opposed to a lecture or speech, is that you are demonstrating or displaying a product or idea; you are showing and explaining something to an audience; you are teaching. A presentation implies visual aids.

Some people get confused and spout ideas such as, "Lincoln didn't need PowerPoint for the Gettysburg Address!" The Gettysburg Address was not a presentation—it was a two-minute **speech.** A speech is generally a formal address or discourse and no one expects you to pull out your laptop. A speech can be five minutes long or several hours long, but it's still a speech, not a presentation.

A **lecture** is educational, but it's usually long and serious and often scholarly and heaven forbid one should have fun with a scholarly lecture. Lectures sometimes come with visual aids such as digital presentations, but then they turn into presentations, not lectures.

So let's keep in mind that if you're going to do a **presentation** (as opposed to a speech or a lecture), you're going to use visual aids. And the point of the visual aids is to *enhance* your talk, not to do it for you.

Does it need to be digital?

Although Apple's Keynote or Microsoft's PowerPoint is the first thing many people think of when they are asked to give a presentation, not all information is best presented digitally. Seriously consider your other alternatives so you know you are using the best method for the information you need to impart.

The method you choose, of course, depends on the number of people in the audience or workshop, the size of the room (a boardroom or a ballroom? a conference room or a classroom?), the time allotment, how many presentations you are giving to this same group, whether you hope to inspire a discussion, the age of the participants, the information you need to get across, etc. You *must* tailor each presentation to its specific audience, its target market.

For very small groups, consider a **flip chart, chalkboard,** or **whiteboard,** along with great handouts. Your skillful use of these tools might thrill your audience because they didn't have to sit through a slide presentation.

And of course, electronic **whiteboards** and **blackboards,** with the appropriate software and connectivity, can send information back and forth between attendees' electronic devices and create an interactive environment.

For any group, even a large one, clear and useful **handouts** can be used instead of slides. This gives attendees something to write on and something to take home. In a large auditorium, there might be people in the group who can't see as well, or the projection system might not be the greatest and consequently the people in the back can't read the slides anyway. When there are charts and data to discuss that just don't present well on an overhead slide, handouts can be a great solution (and of course an *addition* to a visual presentation).

If your presentation is about a book or other object that can be held in the hand, perhaps the **book in everyone's hands** is all you need, referring to specific pages and passages in it.

Many presentations can be **interactive activities** instead. Or perhaps your PowerPoint presentation is just part of the interactivity; if so, is it possible to let go of the PowerPoint part altogether? Maybe all it would take is an extra handout?

Perhaps a **theatrical performance** is what you really want to do, but you feel you have to include a PowerPoint presentation because that's what people expect. So let them experience something new.

Is it possible to involve the **audience** in your visual aids? Never force a reluctant attendee to participate in your presentation, but sometimes members of the audience can hold up signs or images or faces on sticks, stand in as representations of planets revolving around the earth, arrange themselves in the correct levels of the Great Chain of Being, or practice yelling at each other. Generally, the older the group, the fewer audience members who enjoy physically participating, but there are many ways to involve even seniors in low-key ways that help to bring them into the presentation and let you get away without creating something digital.

Remember, even if you have a terrific PowerPoint or Keynote presentation, there is always a chance that the technology might fail and you must fall back on something else. It's a good idea to think about various ways of presenting the same information, just in case.

My personal experience

On the second "Shakespeare at Sea" cruise organized by InsightCruises.com, I was scheduled to provide eight sessions in ten days to the same group of fifty people. How to keep from boring them? You can imagine how deadly it could be if every session were digital slides.

1. "Why Read Shakespeare" was the first presentation. I had discovered on the previous cruise that—gasp—almost all the attendees believed you were only supposed to *watch* the plays and never *read* them yourselves. Apparently only actors have the rocket-science minds to read Shakespeare! So on this cruise I gave a pretty straightforward **digital presentation** about the long history of reading the plays, especially in America, and why we should read them aloud and in groups, preferably. A **handout** provided the outline of my talk along with room for notes.

2. "The Humours" are the four bodily fluids that rise through our bodies as essences and affect our brains. This talk included a **digital presentation** of their importance in the plays, with a time-out halfway through so attendees could take a light-hearted **assessment quiz** (on paper) to see which humour they were most abundant in. Then as I proceeded to discuss the humours of various Shakespearean characters, each attendee knew to which character he or she was most akin. An extensive **handout** included information on how to adjust one's humours, when necessary, when he or she got home.

3. Most attendees were going to see the play *All's Well That Ends Well* later that year. This is one of Shakespeare's least performed plays so few people know the plot, let alone the intricacies. Rather than give a digital presentation or lecture on the play, I edited and occasionally paraphrased (for clarity) the play into a shortened version. I printed up these **play scripts** for everyone, brought props and simple disguises (beards and hats and boas and big rings, etc.), and volunteers read the script aloud in front of the room. I added commentary for clarification, pointed out motifs to watch for, reminders of where the characters were traveling back and forth, someone played the kazoo where the script called for trumpets and fanfare, and so on. By the time we were finished, they felt prepared to see the play and appreciate the subtleties. **No digital presentation at all.**

4. In a **guided discussion** on "Shakespearean Authorship," we looked at the reasons why the issue of authorship is a legitimate concern (it's not because Shakespeare was uneducated and low-born). I provided a two-page **handout** with facts and questions and room for notes. **No digital presentation.**

5. For a presentation on "Death, the Undiscovered Country," I collected a large number of the various mentions of death in the plays and created a small **booklet** for each attendee. We sat in a big double circle. I explained the philosophy of death in Shakespeare's time, the importance of a good death, of "dying well," and then we went around the room reading the quotes and discussing them. **Nothing digital at all.**

6. For a *Macbeth* presentation, I knew the attendees already knew the plot and the big issues. So I created a **digital presentation** as a guideline (some slides of which you can see on pages 58–59), but more importantly, a **handout** with the lines from the play reflecting the various details I was going to talk about—there was too much text to show on a screen and expect everyone to be able to read it. Plus as a handout they could review the lines at home.

7+8. The attendees were also planning to see *Much Ado About Nothing* later that year. Because by this time they had warmed up to reading Shakespeare aloud, we read **scripts** I had brought with me. Some people chose to read along silently, others were happy to take parts. In two two-hour blocks we read the play aloud with some commentary by me and discussion where necessary for clarification. It wasn't scary at all.

I'm only telling you all this to show you examples of using various alternatives to digital slides. Sometimes slides are the perfect media, but always consider alternatives! You want to communicate clearly, whatever you use.

Yes, it needs to be digital

After considering all your options, you often realize that yes, this information would be most effective as a digital, multimedia presentation. So start thinking about how you can use visuals and video and sound to *supplement* you as the speaker. As you read through this book and pull together your ideas, always keep in mind that *you* are the star and your digital presentation is merely your supporting cast; find ways to use that cast appropriately, and don't let it take over and make it unnecessary for you to be there.

A visual example

These are most of the slides from a presentation about how the technologies that have driven the written word have also changed the world. As you can see, *it makes no sense on its own.* You can get a hint of the idea, but all the fascinating details and the intriguing information that pull these disparate ideas together come from my *talk.* The visual presentation *augments* my *talk.* That's a key point to remember as you develop your own presentation—the visuals are merely one piece of the package. The most important part is *you.*

first typefaces based on hand lettering

humanists redesigned the fonts

German black letter

first enterprise

blessed printing machine

and the scribes?

By 1500 15,000,000 books in print

paperback

printing changed the english language

printing killed people

printing furthered religion

Garamond
humanist movement: oldstyle faces

Baskerville
innovation: transitional faces

Bodoni
industrial revolution: modern faces

SNAKE OIL!
advertising: slab serif

rosetta stone

memphis
advertising: slab serif

point system

Linotype

Hot lead can be almost as effective coming from a Linotype as from a firearm.
John O'Hara
Journalist
Linotype

air conditioning

Futura
omigawd: sans serif

Marconi
digital type

Linotype

macintosh computer

macintosh computer

ibm pc (QDOS)

The Mac
Aldus PageMaker
Canon engine
Postcript
page description language
four technologies

THE WALL
type in the hands of the masses

escaliDo
type in the hands of the masses

the web

the web

the web

Thank you!

What's a bad presentation?

Once you have given your first presentation, you become keenly aware of what others do that enhance or spoil a presentation in varying degrees. Make notes of these. Here are a few things that can make your audience less than thrilled about your time on stage:

The structure

Lack of preparation

Disorganization

Boring content

Too much information

Not focused for this audience

The presenter

Mumbling, shouting, verbal clutter (um, uh, I mean, you know, etc.), or a monotonous tone of voice

Monotonous pace or moving too fast

Shuffling through papers

Unfamiliar with the technology

Talking in the dark

Standing at a podium directly in front of the screen

Rarely (or never) looking at the audience

Reading from a paper or from the screen

The digital presentation itself

Overabundance of annoying transitions, silly doodads, and irrelevant animation

Dorky clip art

Small text on the screen

Huge amount of small text on the screen

Inconsistent look and feel: different font on every slide, different arrangement on every slide

What's a good presentation?

We'll get into specific design features of what makes a digital presentation *look* good in later chapters. But every presentation leaves the audience with a good, neutral, or bad feeling, no matter what it looks like. What is it that creates a good impression? Obviously, most important is a lack of the annoying things listed on the opposite page, but also consider:

Interesting content, of course (how 'bout that)

Content tailored to the specific audience

Clear and simple organization

Few bullet points

Visuals that are *relevant* to the content and the audience

Animation that enhances content and is not distracting

Information in the *talk* is more than what is shown on the *screen*

A connection to the audience, the feeling of a conversation

Practiced performance (and this *is* a performance)

Humor is always great, if possible

Put it in words

You've been to good and bad presentations. **Put into words** what it is that you liked about good ones and what was not effective in the not-so-good ones. Sometimes a presentation might be great in a lot of ways and just off in one or two little things. Make note of that.

Once you can put into words what the problem or the solution is, you are much more conscious of it and can work with it. If all you can say is, "Mmm, it was boring," you're not going to learn anything. *Why* was it boring? What *specifically* made it boring? By taking the time to formulate words and pinpoint the issues, you can avoid doing the annoying things in your own presentations and work on incorporating the positive elements.

Software options

For digital presentations, there are four main options.

Microsoft PowerPoint

There are various price levels depending on which version of Microsoft Office you buy (the home/student version, the professional, Mac or PC, etc.) and whether you buy PowerPoint alone or the entire suite (it's actually cheaper to buy the suite). See page 14. PowerPoint is the most ubiquitous presentation software, but all the others can open PowerPoint presentations and sometimes save in that format as well.

Apple Keynote

Keynote is part of the Apple iWork package that also includes Pages (a word processor/page layout application) and Numbers (a spreadsheet app). The cost for the package of three applications is $79, and it's only available for the Mac. See the opposite page.

Keynote can open PowerPoint files. It can also save files in the PowerPoint format so they can be viewed on a PC, but you'll lose a number of features in the process, so be sure to test the result before you show the presentation.

Google Presently

This is part of Google's online documents package. It's free and can be used as a collaborative tool. See page 15.

OpenOffice Impress

This software is available for computers running the Macintosh operating system, Windows, or Linux. And it's free. See page 16.

If you use a Mac and you have a choice, use Keynote—it has the most features and is the easiest to use. If you have a PC, PowerPoint is probably your default application, but you can also use Google Presently or OpenOffice Impress (both free).

Apple Keynote

Keynote provides dozens of beautiful templates so you can get straight to work. If you have a me.com account with Apple, you can share the presentation online and give invited users the options to post comments on each page, write notes for others, and even download the file. Check it out at Apple.com/iWork.

Microsoft PowerPoint

You probably already own PowerPoint if you have a PC.

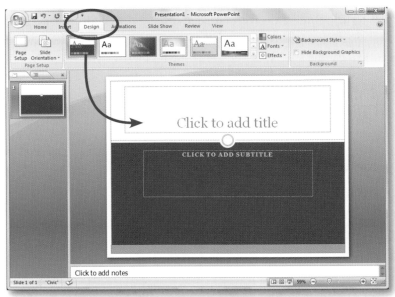

This is one of the Windows versions of PowerPoint. Yours might look a little different depending on how old it is and which version it is. Get the latest.

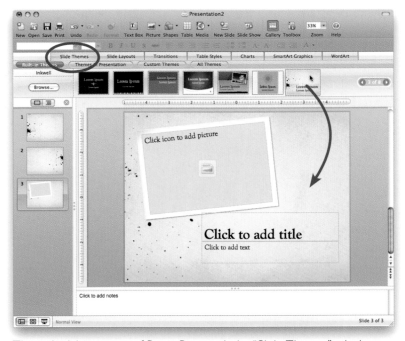

This is the Mac version of PowerPoint with the "Slide Themes" tab showing.

Google Presently

Google Docs at docs.Google.com has a presentation web application called Presently. You must have a Google account (which is free) to open and share a presentation. You can create, edit, and share presentations with coworkers, friends, or family; people to whom you give permission can work on them as well, simultaneously, so it functions as a collaborative tool. You can import .ppt files (PowerPoint) and .pps (PowerPoint slideshow viewer) files; download your presentations as PDFs, .ppt, or text files; and publish or embed them on web pages for the world to see.

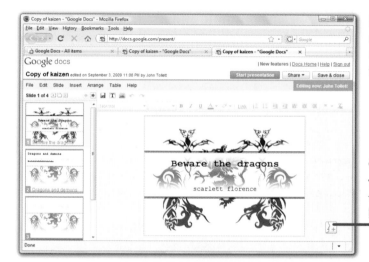

Presently on Windows, using a free template.

Click here to write or read the "Speaker Notes."

Presently on a Mac, using a free template.

Click here to write or read the "Speaker Notes."

OpenOffice Impress

Impress isn't as sexy as Keynote, but it's free. If you're a pretty good designer, you can create nice-looking presentations. You only get one style of transition between all slides, and other features are much more limited than Keynote or PowerPoint, but what do you expect for free?

Impress can save in PowerPoint format and can be used on a Mac, a Windows machine, or with Linux. Download it at www.OpenOffice.org.

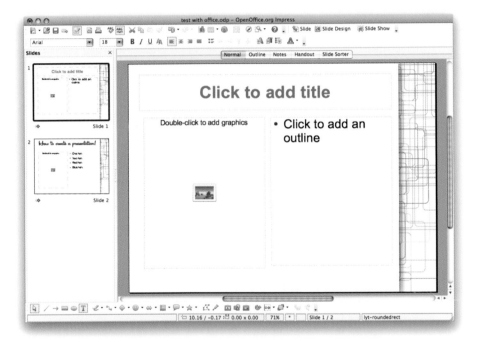

2 Get yourself organized

Some people like to jump right in to the software and start laying out the slides; others prefer to spend some time getting their thoughts organized.

I, too, love to jump right in to the software, but I have to admit that by doing so I get bogged down in what the presentation looks like much too soon and end up redesigning the whole thing several times as I add more content. So I've learned to control myself and get organized *first*.

Once you've got the data organized, then you can use the four guidelines in the next section to clarify the information; find relevant graphics, video, or sound; consider appropriate animation that will help reveal the information, and pull your thoughts together into a cohesive unit with a beginning, middle, and end.

Plan, organize, outline

Perhaps organization is one of your strong points and thus you feel perfectly competent in developing your presentation; maybe you even have some preferred tools and methods. You're lucky, because organization is one of the most important foundations for a successful presentation.

Or maybe you've got all kinds of ideas flying around in your head and need some way to focus them. You're lucky too, because there are several tools available to help you harness your ideas.

First of all, if you're using Keynote or PowerPoint, make sure you find the "Outline" mode (see page 20). It allows you to type headlines and bullet points without worrying about what the project looks like. Trying to design the presentation at the same time you're organizing it can get you sidetracked, so the outline mode lets you focus on just that one thing—organization.

BUT before you even start the outline, whether you are a natural organizer or not, I strongly suggest you read Chapter 3 so you can avoid the sin of writing your presentation onto the slides, which then forces you to read your slides. At the most, you want a heading or a few words on the screen that alerts the audience to what you will be *talking* about, and your notes can go in the "Presenter Notes" area of your software, as shown below.

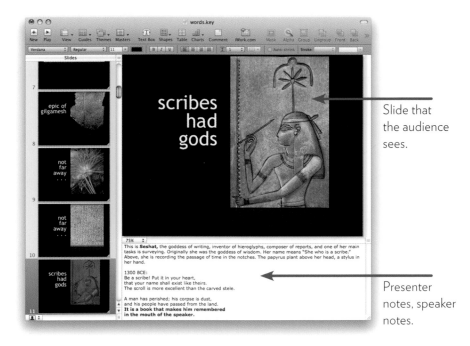

Slide that the audience sees.

Presenter notes, speaker notes.

Old technology Post-it Notes

In these days of technology for everything, don't neglect good ol' Post-it Notes. It's wonderfully easy to scribble notes by hand and move them around on the table or the wall. Any kind of sticky notes work great as a simple collaborative tool as well. And their size forces you to limit the number of words per heading.

This is an example of my preparation for a presentation, before opening the software. I wrote on lots of sticky notes, cut out important points from a paper I had written and pasted those in position, etc., while organizing the information. I like to see the whole thing visually.

Outline features in presentation software

PowerPoint and Keynote have outline views in which you can create the structure of your presentation in plain text and not worry about what it looks like yet. If you've ever worked with the outline feature in your word processor, you'll feel very comfortable with this.

As you can see below, in the outline you can type up your thoughts as quickly as you can think; at any time, grab the tiny slide icon (not the text) and drag that slide to another position to rearrange it.

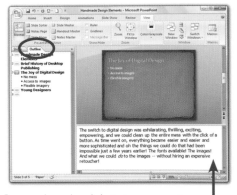

Remember, the slide is to augment your *talk.* Write your talking points in the speaker notes area, *not* on the slide.

Consider opening the outline area so wide that you can see very little of the slide—it keeps you from being distracted by the visuals.

OmniOutliner software (Mac only) takes the outline form to a higher level, so if you like to work in outline mode, go to OmniGroup.com and check it out. You can organize topics, subtopics (bullet points) and speaker notes with greater flexibility and more options, then export your file as a Keynote presentation. It can even import presentations that you've already started in Keynote. OmniOutliner is inexpensive, and you can download a trial version (it might be on your Mac already—check your Applications folder).

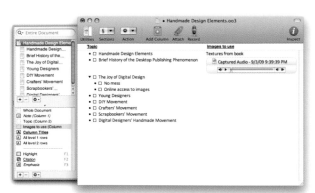

With OmniOutliner, you can also organize the multimedia files in your presentation.

Mind maps and idea clouds

If you like to use concept maps, mind maps, idea clouds, or idea webs (all of which are variations on a visual representation of your outline) to develop your project graphically instead of textually/linearly, check out Inspiration software (Inspiration.com, Mac and Windows, $69). It's a great tool for outlining in a visual way, as shown below. You can insert multimedia files, and even record your voice directly in the application.

Inspiration can take your visual concept map and create a standard outline in text form where you can drag and drop items to rearrange them. You can export the outline to a word processor or as a PowerPoint presentation. Inspiration also makes Webspiration for collaborating online.

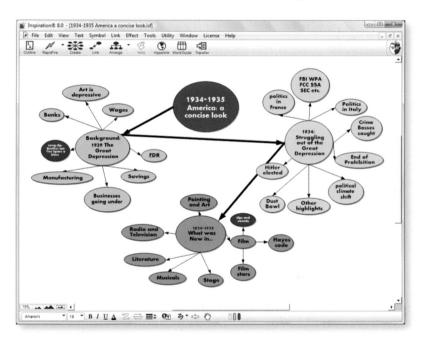

Slide sorter or light table view in software

Once you've got some slides to work with, you can check the overall structure in the "Slide Sorter" view in PowerPoint or the "Light Table" view in Keynote. This is a great place to take a look at all the slides in your presentation and see how the organization is progressing. You can drag slides around to reorganize them.

presentation researched and created by Ross Carter

Once you start *designing* the slides, this Slide Sorter or Light Table view will help you see where you need to be more consistent, which slides need more contrast, whether the type size is large or bold enough, etc. Take advantage of this great feature.

FOUR
principles of
CONCEPTUAL
PRESENTATION
Design

OPTIMIZE THE CONTENT

Before you begin to design the *visual* look of your slides, spend some time preparing the content *conceptually*. If you give some thought to the ideas in this section, it will be easier to design the actual slides, and you'll have a fuller, richer presentation.

Four principles of **conceptual** presentation design

In *The Non-Designer's Design Book* I narrowed down the time-honored principles of design into four basic ideas: contrast, repetition, alignment, and proximity. In the section following this one, I'll repeat those principles again as applied specifically to presentation slides.

But before we actually design the slides, let's go over four principles you need to consider *before you begin the design process.* These principles will give you things to think about as you start putting your project together.

Clarity

Can the clutter. Get to the point. Simplify. Be specific. Edit. You don't have to tell them *everything.* Open up the text— don't cram all the information together.

Relevance

Don't confuse the issues with irrelevant stuff on the slide or in the talk. Relate ideas and graphics to your topic, as well as to that *particular* audience. Also, everything you say and how you say it should relate to who *you* are and why you're there.

Animation

Understand how to take advantage of *relevant* animation and transitions to *clarify* your information, not to confuse it.

Plot

Tell the story. Define the path you plan to take and why you're going there. Start at the beginning and stop at the end. If the project warrants it, build it up to a climax (then wind down and get out). Inject some humanity into your presentation. *Talk* to your audience.

If you have these ideas in your mind before you begin, you'll create a presentation that your audience will enjoy experiencing.

Clarity

This chapter encourages you to make sure your presentation is clear and understandable and that viewers can easily assimilate your information. No matter how pretty you make it, all that prettiness is worthless if you aren't communicating clearly.

Part of communicating clearly is deciding what should be left out. It's a difficult struggle to edit out information that you think is important. But keep in mind that no one in your audience is going to remember *everything* you say, and actually, the less you say, the more they will remember. Prioritize the information *for this particular audience* and delete items that take away from the primary focus. For instance, do the sales reps really need a history of the corporation and its mission statement, or can you get right to the point and show the demo they need? (Give them a link to the corporate overview on the handout or brochure you leave behind.)

Edit the text!

The possibilities for a clean, streamlined, visually pleasant presentation are enhanced with good editing. Get rid of those extra words! The fewer words on the slide, the larger the words can be and the more design options you have.

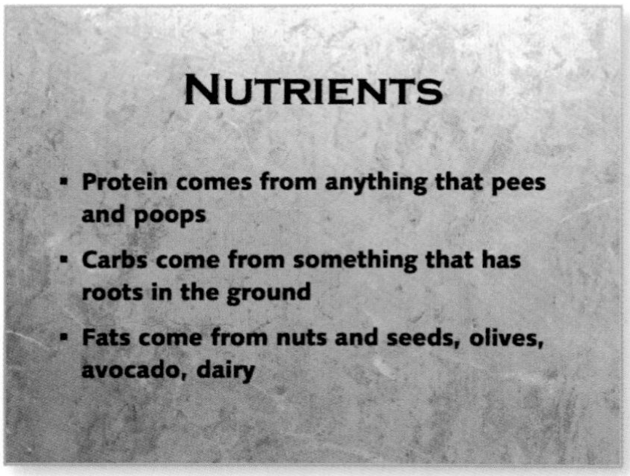

NUTRIENTS

- Protein comes from anything that pees and poops
- Carbs come from something that has roots in the ground
- Fats come from nuts and seeds, olives, avocado, dairy

By editing out all the superfluous words (above), the presenter had more room (below) to add contrast, make the type bigger, and provide a clearer message for quick reading and notetaking.

Condensing the information to its essentials also makes it easier for you to present because you can use the slides as quick reference points to keep you on track.

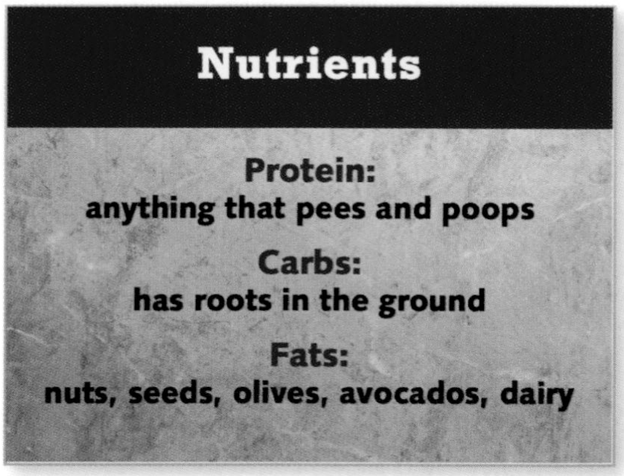

Nutrients

Protein:
anything that pees and poops

Carbs:
has roots in the ground

Fats:
nuts, seeds, olives, avocados, dairy

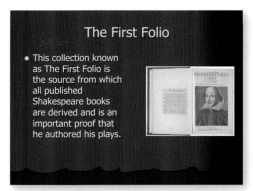

In this example, the instructor has too many words on the page. Most of the words are actually useless because he is going to spend several minutes talking about this object, the First Folio.

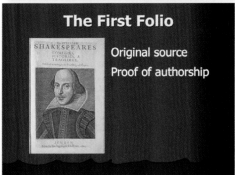

By condensing the key points into a few words, he makes it easier for students to grasp the points and to fill in their notes with more information while still listening to the instructor. And he can enlarge both the graphic (cropped) and the text.

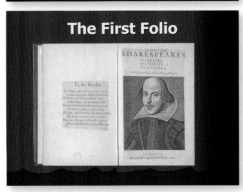

He might consider not using any bullet points at all on the slide, just a visual of the First Folio. The image and its title will stick in the students' minds much longer than the text with too many unnecessary words.

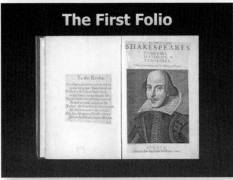

And I would recommend getting rid of that silly background. If you're going to use an evocative background, make sure you work with it—don't just plop things on top of it.

Avoid lengthy complete sentences

You rarely need to write complete sentences, especially if they're long. You will be *speaking* in complete sentences, so you want your audience to be able to skim the main points on your slide. If the main points are instantly accessible (if no one has to sludge through a dense sentence), the audience can immediately grasp the ideas on the slide and still have enough brain-processing power left over to *listen* to you as you elaborate on those points.

Notice in the example below there are no bullets. There are bullet *points,* but simply eliminating the actual bullets softens the slide.

Anger Management

There are positive aspects of anger in that you have increased energy, you are able to communicate your feelings, able to problem solve, and you can take charge of the situation.

http://www.angermanage.org/question_show.cfm?selected=9

5

Anger Management

Positive aspects of anger:

Can explain your feelings,

solve problems,

take charge of situations,

increase your energy

I also got rid of unnecessary items on the slide. Important web addresses (as on the slide above) should be on your handouts—no one can copy complex addresses properly while listening to you.

With this limited amount of text, you can speak your piece and your audience will pick up these main points more easily.

Don't present your notes

Below is an example of the kind of presentation that makes people holler, "Don't read your slides!" The problem is not that the speaker reads her slide—the problem is that she has put her introductory notes right on the slide *so she has no choice but to read the slide*—it's her intro.

This style of presentation design is perfectly okay if you plan to post the file and it must stand alone. But if you are presenting it in person, do not put the full text *that you plan to say* on the page. Otherwise why do you need to show up?

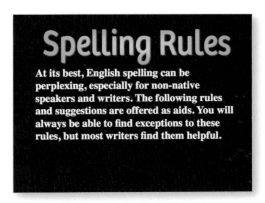

Don't write on the slide what you plan to speak aloud. Give people a reason to listen to your dynamic self.

This is all you need for an intro slide. You'll **show** this slide and **speak** the text as shown above.

By *not* reading the slide, it emphasizes YOU as the authority and center of this presentation. It indicates that you know your stuff and are comfortable speaking and teaching, not just reading.

Write in the active voice

I realize this little reminder about active voice vs. passive voice is not really a design issue, but it will affect the number of words you put on a slide, which *is* a design issue. I bring it up right here because generally the active voice takes fewer words and right now we're in the process of deleting superfluous words for clarity.

You can recognize when a sentence is in passive voice because no one is responsible. It's like when you're talking to a group about an issue but don't want to point fingers.

> "The office microwave was blown up by someone" is passive.
> "George blew up the microwave" is active.

On a slide, if you see that you explain or give directions passively, make those directions active.

> "When a fire is suspected, one can push the Big Red Button"
> is passive.
> "If you suspect a fire, push the Big Red Button" is active.

> "If you have the feeling that your life is being threatened,
> you can often escape by running away" is passive.
> "If your life is threatened, run" is active.

Active writing is more dynamic and, more importantly for a slide presentation, *it uses fewer words.*

The passive voice uses too many words:

With fewer words, you can consider using full-screen graphics. You are going to be expanding on this topic as you speak (that's why you're there) so you don't need all those words on the screen:

Now try even fewer words:

Images are from iStockphoto.com

You can consider not using any text at all, since your attendees will have a visual message in their eyes and your relevant words in their ears (and any necessary tables of data in their handouts; see Chapter 13). It's very trendy to do that right now—images with no words. But having the key word or phrase *plus* the image is a perfectly viable option because it brands *both* the text and the image into the brain and there's nothing wrong with that. And the phrase on the screen helps you easily refer to items as you talk about them.

Avoid the 'ings

Gerunds are those verbs that act as nouns or noun phrases by adding "ing" to them. 'Ings tend to be passive and weak, and it takes more words to use 'ings.

"Do you mind my *asking*?" as opposed to, "May I ask?"

"There is *going* to be hell to pay," as opposed to,
"There will be hell to pay."

"We will be *seeing* a drop in sales next week," as opposed to,
"Sales will drop next week."

"You're *going* to make my day," as opposed to
"Make my day."

Check your text and see if you can delete any gerunds and thus make the sentences or phrases more direct, less passive, and use fewer words.

Sometimes, of course, a word ending in 'ing is the best possible word to use, and that's okay. For instance, you can't talk about the fishing industry without using the word "fishing." The "fish industry" just isn't right.

But get rid of the 'ings that are unnecessary.

Anger Management	Anger Management
Anger management would be seen then as increasing the positive aspects or functions of anger and decreasing the negative functions of anger.	Increases the positive functions of anger Decreases the negative functions of anger

By getting rid of the complete sentence and getting rid of the 'ings, the message is much clearer.

Also, can you see how passive that sentence is? "Anger management would be seen then as . . . ." Good heavens, how wimpy can you get? Stand up and make a statement: "Anger management increases the positive functions of anger." There.

With fewer words on the slide, the audience can easily listen to you, take notes, and still absorb the important content.

Experiment with editing the text

All of the preceding guidelines are designed to shorten your text so you 1) have more design options, 2) don't bore your audience, 3) provide greater clarity, and 4) allow your audience to focus on you and what you're saying instead of trying to read a lot of words.

Below are examples of slides that contain too much text. Can you edit them down so they contain the essential information? Keep in mind that *the slides should not tell the entire story, they are not expected to stand on their own.*

Also keep in mind that as a presenter, you usually have an obligation to provide handouts for your attendees (see Chapter 13 on handouts). Even when you post a presentation online, you can include the speaker notes. Consider what text should be on the screen as opposed to in your talk and in your handouts. Some possible editing solutions are on the following page.

Shakespeare the Chaucerian

- Chaucerian influence is rife throughout the Shakespearean canon.
- Shakespeare reads Chaucer closely and engages him in a variety of subtle ways, often responding to some issue Chaucer posits or providing his own reaction to a particular theme.
- Shakespeare displays a deep understanding and appreciation for Chaucer's art and methods.

THE MIGHTY APOSTROPHE

The apostrophe has only a handful of uses, but these uses are very important. A misplaced apostrophe can be annoying — not to mention lonely. The apostrophe is used to create possessives, to show contractions, and to create some plural forms.

Below are two examples of the editing possibilities, and certainly not the *only* possibilities. Notice I also made some design decisions along the way to help improve the clarity. We'll be looking at the design of a slide more carefully in the next section, but right now, can you point out the differences in the looks?

Shakespeare the Chaucerian

- Chaucer influenced Shakespeare
- Shakespeare read Chaucer closely
- The plays show deep understanding and appreciation

Each of these topics requires the presenter to elaborate. By editing the text, the audience can more clearly see where he is heading and can more easily follow along.

Consider deleting the bullets as well.

The Mighty Apostrophe

A handful of important uses

Misplaced apostrophes are annoying

This presenter made the common mistake of typing his introduction right on the screen so then he ends up reading it. I eliminated his entire last sentence because that should be another slide altogether, after he gets through his intro.

A good presentation revolves around you, the person, not around your slides. So don't replace yourself with text on slides; don't make yourself redundant!

Sometimes you need the text

I'm not giving you rules such as, "Never use more than five bullets" or "Never use more than three words per bullet point" or "Never use more than six words per slide." What I am doing is promoting **CLARITY.** Sometimes that means you need more text. *If you need more text to provide absolute clarity, then use more text.*

Quoting someone else provides a good example of the necessity of enough words. Quotes are great—they are succinct, usually clever or we wouldn't be quoting them, and can add credibility to our own talking points. But how many quotes are six words or less?

And unless you positively *know* that every person in the entire auditorium has great eyesight (or can even see in the first place), read that quote aloud. You are probably doing that already and maybe feeling guilty because you're always told not to read your slides aloud, but phooey on that (as I mentioned on page 29, that's a misinterpreted guideline). Reading the quote aloud does a service to those who can't see well, plus it reinforces the message when it goes in eyes and ears at the same time, plus you create a connection between *you* and the clever person you are quoting. And your message will be clearer.

If I had more time, I would have written a shorter letter.

t.s. eliot

Mr. Eliot understood how difficult it is to write less.

I suppose this slide could say:

   More time = shorter letter

but then it would be a data point and we'd miss the human being struggling with this thought.

Spread out the text!

I'm not sure why presenters so often feel compelled to put all their bullet points on one slide. Slides are free. Six slides or a hundred slides—it costs the same! So spread out your message. You might want to give an overview on one slide, for instance, of the next five points you are going to focus on, but then repeat each focus point *on a separate slide* so your audience can read the slide and take notes on just that one important point. Remember, the point of your presentation is to communicate information clearly, so present it clearly.

Prosody Assignment

- Using the three copies of your Shakespearean sonnet, do each of the following.
  1. Scan the poem for **Meter-divide the poem into feet and mark stressed and unstressed syllables and label the variations**
  2. Analyze the poem for **Alliteration-mark similar consonant sounds**
  3. Analyze the poem for **Assonance-mark similar vowel sounds**

There is too much text and it's too dense. A student has to struggle through the sentences word by word, and surely the instructor is talking while the student is reading.

First, ***get rid of*** Arial/Helvetica. It just reeks of boring (see page 140 if you really want to use it).

(***And get rid of*** the hyphens where they don't belong—it's confusing and they're wrong: "Meter-divide" is not a hyphenated word.)

Prosody Assignment

- Using the three copies of your Shakespearean sonnet, do the following.
  1. Scan the poem for **Meter: divide the poem into feet and mark stressed and unstressed syllables and label the variations**
  2. Analyze the poem for **Alliteration: mark similar consonant sounds**
  3. Analyze the poem for **Assonance: mark similar vowel sounds**

This slide instantly has a nicer look with the new font, and the important points are highlighted in blue. ***But it's still too heavy and dense.***

Get rid of the superfluous words. Since you, as instructor, are going to elaborate on each of the three tasks, eliminate unnecessary words from this slide so students instantly see what their three tasks are.

Prosody Assignment

- Using the three copies of your Shakespearean sonnet, do the following.
  1. Scan the poem for **Meter**
  2. Analyze the poem for **Alliteration**
  3. Analyze the poem for **Assonance**

Clarity. Yes. As a student, now I know exactly what to write in my notes and I know exactly what my tasks are.

1. Scan for Meter

- Divide the poem into feet
- Mark stressed and unstressed syllables
- Label the variations

Now each task is explained. I can clearly see what each task entails, and I can write clear notes.

As the instructor proceeds to elaborate and answer questions, I can focus—without struggling to decipher dense text on the screen at the same time.

2. Analyze for Alliteration

- Mark similar consonant sounds at the beginnings of words

3. Analyze for Assonance

- Mark similar vowel sounds inside of words

Use all the slides you need

Here is another example along the same lines—why put all five bullet points on one slide? Your attendees will be trying to write down all five of these as soon as you start talking about the first one. Give them one principle at a time—they can write that one down quickly (or add notes to their handout), then give you their undivided attention. Everyone is happier.

A GOOD WEIGHT MANAGEMENT PROGRAM

- Has a good balance of protein, carbohydrates, and fat
- Meets your individual daily requirements of nutrients (proteins, carbs & fats)
- Includes protein at each meal
- Does not exclude food groups
- Helps you understand the emotional impact of your eating

One result of displaying all five bullet points on one slide is that the type has to be so small.

Plus your audience has too much to worry about and will not be able to catch all the information.

You could make your bullet points zoom in from the side one at a time, but why do that when slides are free? Make more slides!

A Good Weight Management Program

Has five aspects:

12345

By using more slides, we can make the text larger on each one, focus on each point, and have more room to add contrast to the page in the bargain.

This intro slide leads into the following five slides.

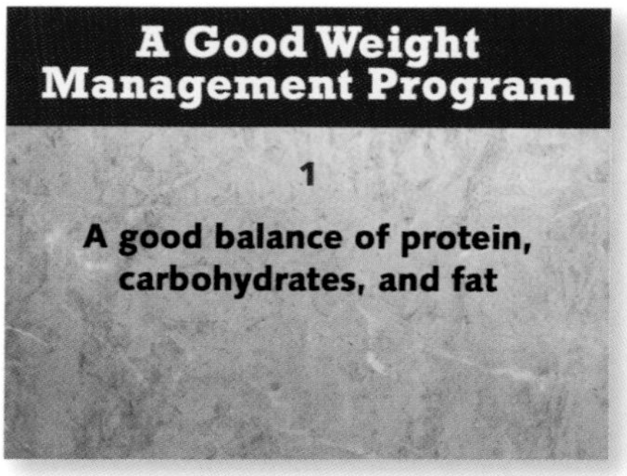

A Good Weight Management Program

1

A good balance of protein, carbohydrates, and fat

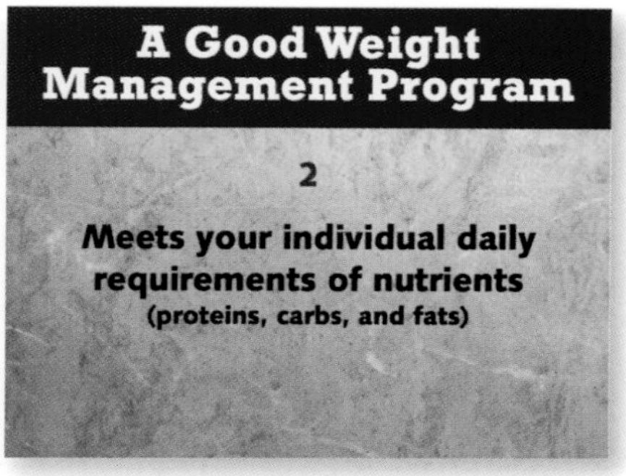

A Good Weight Management Program

2

Meets your individual daily requirements of nutrients
(proteins, carbs, and fats)

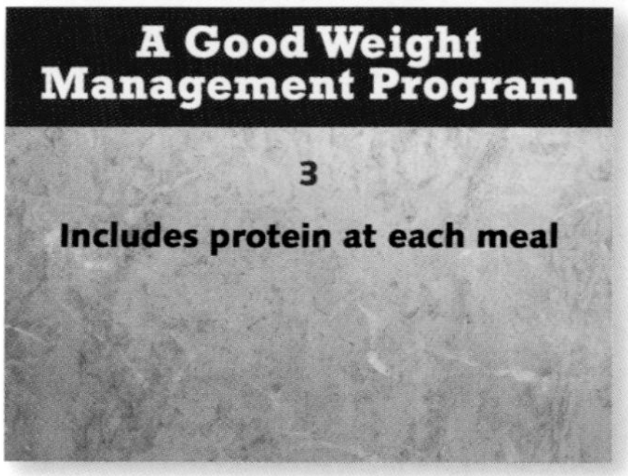

A Good Weight Management Program

3

Includes protein at each meal

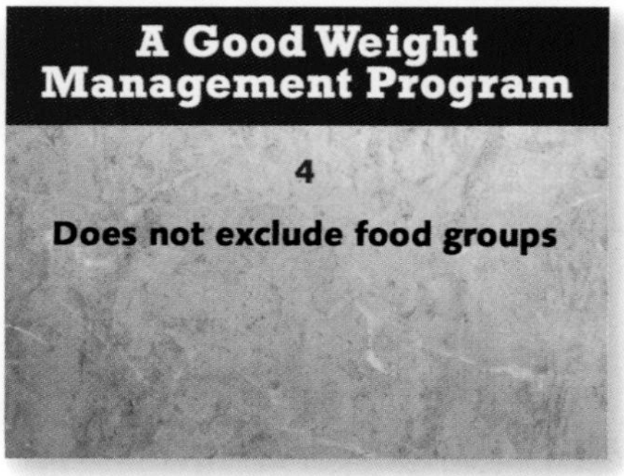

A Good Weight Management Program

4

Does not exclude food groups

The presenter will elaborate on each of these points. Thus the attendees can add to their notes calmly and clearly.

Notice there are no bullets at all.

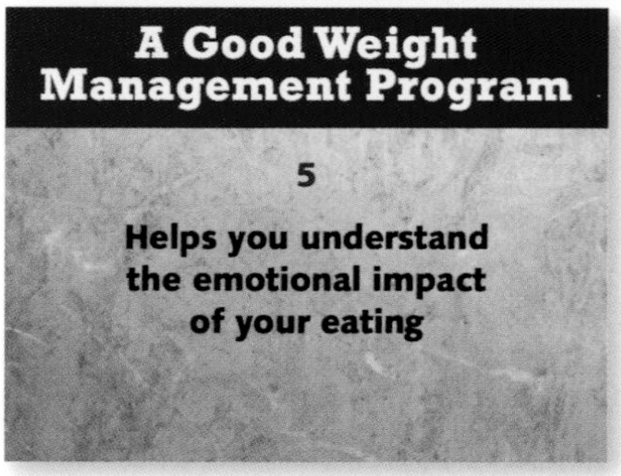

A Good Weight Management Program

5

Helps you understand the emotional impact of your eating

Whether you put all your bullet points on one slide (left) or each on individual slides (below), it will take the same amount of time to talk about them. On individual slides, it is easier for your audience to see, follow, understand, and take notes. And it's easier to look at.

(This is a Keynote template.)

How many slides in a presentation?

I realize some presentation gurus make up rules about how many slides you should have in a presentation. Let's say your presentation uses 46 slides and it's neat and organized and takes just the right amount of time. Someone tells you, "Oh no! A good presentation has no more than 18 slides! It's a RULE!" So you cram all your information onto 18 slides. It still takes the same amount of time! But now it has a cluttered visual impression and is difficult to comprehend—it lacks clarity.

It's not the number of slides that makes the difference. It's your organization and personal presentation of that material that makes the difference.

If you have a lot of slides, be sure to read pages 60–61 about transitions to help your audience follow along with your changes in topics.

Also see pages 70–71 about varying your pace as you go through slides so it's not a monotonous production.

photo by Jim Thomas

Do you see anything odd on this slide?

It insists that there be "fewer than 5 words per slide." A bit ironic, eh?

I'm also a little confused about the relevance of the photo. Yes, it's a "high-impact graphic," but what's its point in this presentation? One part of my mind is trying to listen to the speaker and another part is trying to make a connection between the words and the image. Don't confuse me!

But use one slide when appropriate!

Keep in mind I'm not recommending that every little topic be on a separate slide. Of course there are many times when one slide is sufficient for a number of bulleted items (even if you don't actually use a bullet). Generally, when you have a group of items that you might be skimming over or introducing or talking about as a collection, keep them on one slide.

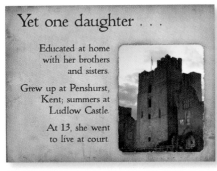

Each of these topics about Mary Sidney's childhood are closely related and only take a minute for each bullet point, so I left them all on one slide.

While discussing a tragic time in her life, each bullet slides in from the left as I bring it up. Because they are so related and I want the audience to see the cumulative list of grief, they are all on one slide.

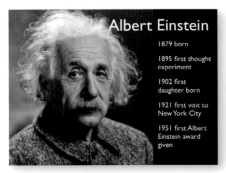

If all of your talking points are about one thing and you won't be dwelling on specific items, then of course leave your bullets on one page; bring them on one at a time if you prefer. Only expand into more pages if your **talk** expands on those items.

images from commons.WikiMedia.org

As you develop your presentation, you'll figure out whether or not to leave all your items on one page or to expand into multiple slides. By grouping some items and expanding others, it will help you to vary the pace of the presentation—some slides go by quickly, some you linger on, some prompt further discussion; it's like a conversation among friends.

Sometimes you *need* a lot on one slide

It's just a fact with presentations that sometimes you do need a lot on the screen. It might be a complex chart, a comparison of diagrams, or an important progression of tasks. Or your presentation might be intended as a stand-alone piece that gets distributed and so you'll have much more on the screen than if you were giving the talk in person. This is where it is *most* important to be clear and uncluttered, both in the text and in the design.

And don't forget that even when a presentation is distributed throughout the office or posted online, there is always a place for speaker notes.

Let's take a look at a very busy slide and see what we can do to make it clearer.

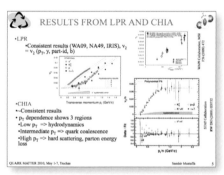

This is the original slide. Look at every object and see if there are any that are unnecessary.

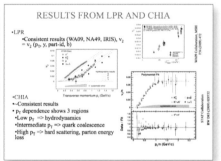

It's surely safe to remove the dorky clip art from the top corners, yes? And we can make an argument that the slide number in the bottom right can go, and even the footer text since that information is on the first and last slides and in the handout.

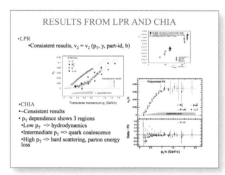

Not much of the other text can be removed, so we'll have to work with that (see the following page).

I can't imagine (although that doesn't mean it's not possible) that one could give this presentation or distribute these slides without an accompanying handout or speaker notes. You must admit that in the original slide, no one in the room would be able to read the data on these charts or be able to visually compare their results. So let's bite the bullet and separate the charts onto individual slides. If you're giving this presentation live, it's not difficult to flip back and forth between these three slides to show comparisons, and if they get printed, now the reader can actually see what they're looking at.

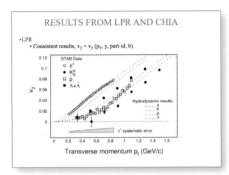

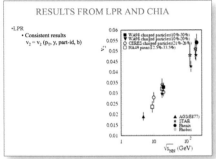

These slides still need some work (particularly alignment), but at least the data is usable now. Slides are free—don't be afraid to use as many as you need to present the information clearly.

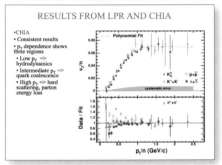

Are you worried that when you print your slides with notes using the default option in your software, too many pages will have to be printed? Then buck up and create an appropriate handout instead of relying on the software to do it for you.

Clarity in the design

I'm a firm believer that the visual *look* of the material is as important to **clarity** as what the material *says*. In the next section (not the next chapter) I'll talk about how to design clarity into your slides, but you can't do that unless you've first made sure the information itself is clear and succinct.

4 Relevance

Everything you put on your slide should be **relevant** to the topic of that slide *and* to your audience. This includes not only the text, but the graphics and backgrounds.

Remember, the point of your presentation is to communicate something clearly. The more irrelevant items you have on your slides, the more it takes attention away from you and the more difficult it is for your audience to mentally sift through the pieces and combine them into a coherent whole, all the while trying to listen to you.

And keep in mind that what is relevant to one audience might not be to another. Does the conservative, older audience really want the loud and naughty video bits that are in the presentation for a younger and wilder crowd?

Part of the clarity and relevance of the information develops from your commitment to do your homework—you cannot create one presentation to show to six different markets. You might, however, create one master presentation with everything you want to say about this topic, and then make six copies of that master to **customize each one for an individual market.** Your thoughtfulness and care will show, and it will impress your audience.

Get rid of superfluous stuff

You don't need all kinds of gewgaws sitting on your slide cluttering up your information. Don't stick random rubbish in the corners—the corners really don't mind being empty! The more stuff you stick on the screen that has nothing to do with your presentation, the more you disrupt the focus. If the focus is visually disrupted, it translates into your audience losing focus.

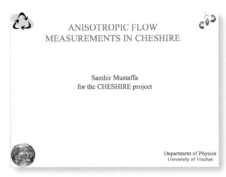

As you look at this slide, be conscious of your eye movement. How many times does your eye have to move from place to place to make sure you see everything?

As a viewer, how long does it take before you feel confident that you've absorbed all the information on this slide? Imagine trying to process that while listening to someone talk about anisotropic flow measurements.

A shovel? I have to dig my own foundation? There's buried treasure? You're a gravedigger? Don't you find your mind trying to make a connection between the shovel and the information?

Hmm, on this slide about developing a business plan, I'm a little confused by the astronomy imagery and a drafting table with sparkles. Really, it's better to have no graphics at all than irrelevant graphics that take the viewer's mind in the wrong direction. And please don't fill the white space with random objects like lines. It's okay to have empty space. *It's okay.*

That includes the logo on every page

I realize that some presenters believe strongly that every darn slide in the entire deck should have at least one company logo on it, or perhaps two logos, or a logo and a tag line, or a logo and a company name and a tag line. You've got people trapped in a room for an hour and they have no choice but to look at the screen, so why not brand your brand into their brains?

Is the point to make sure they don't forget who you are? Hmm, wouldn't the audience be more inclined to remember you if 1) your presentation is great, and 2) the handouts *they take back to their offices* are terrific and useful and nice-looking so they will be kept and not trashed? *It is on your useful handout* that your corporate logo belongs, not on the ephemeral slide.

After a few slides that logo becomes simply clutter and the brains of attendees blank out its meaning.

One logo on every slide. No, two logos on every slide. Combine that with the unnecessary background picture, the blue edges taking up space, and the horizontal line. If we take out everything that's *irrelevant*, perhaps we can make the type big enough to read. If this slideshow is presented in person, the "References" page is a total waste of time; if that information is important, put it in the handout.

Personally, I still think there's too much text on these pages (if it's a live presentation) and the statistics could use more interesting treatment (perhaps with images of actual humans), but at least we've gotten rid of the irrelevant pieces and can start to work from here. After you read Chapter 9 on Alignment and Chapter 10 on Repetition, come back to this page and notice those differences in the sets of slides.

Brand with your colors, your typography, your inimitable style, your critical information, your useful handout. Not with a logo on every slide.

Backgrounds

A great deal of the visual impression of your presentation comes from the background you choose, so choose it carefully. If you can't find a template that suits your material, there are lots of graphic tools in your software to create your own background. You can also invest a few dollars in images from a vendor such as iStockphoto.com.

There are two important things to remember, based on the number of bad slides I've seen:

> Choose a background that *complements* your talk, one that is *relevant* to it, not a background that *contradicts* or *confuses* it.

> *Work with the background*—don't just randomly pile stuff on it.

Below-left you see the actual opening slide as the presenter created it; on the right, I added a nice background image that I bought for $3 at iStockphoto. com, and I invested in an interesting and relevant font (Apocrypha from FontShop.com) instead of the default Arial. You can see what a dramatic difference it makes, and you can imagine the difference in the audience's immediate perception.

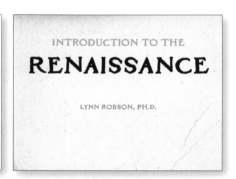

You will learn in the next section that all I did with the type in the way of design was to add contrast—a contrast of the size of font and a contrast of color.

Don't be afraid to put your name on the introductory slide—your audience *wants* to know who you are.

Hmm, a presentation about purchasing a home on a background of the open ocean. My brain, all through the speaker's talk, will be constantly trying to process the connection between the ocean and a suburban house.

Here's a guideline to remember: *If it looks hard to read, it is.* This example is hard to read even on your computer, so please consider how much more difficult it will be on a screen in a large room. Besides making the text difficult to read, this irrelevant background does nothing to clarify the topic.

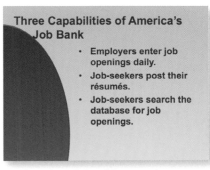 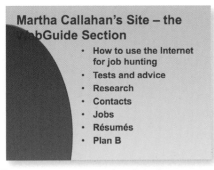

I realize that it's hard for new designers to allow empty space on the slide, but you must learn to let it be there. This random shape, apparently used to take up blank space, is totally irrelevant and is so random that the slide creator can't figure out how to integrate the text with it. In the next section, I'll give you some guidelines about where to place both text and images. For now, get rid of irrelevant backgrounds and images.

I recognize that part of the ubiquitous problem of inappropriate backgrounds and their use is that Microsoft (and many third parties) provides free PowerPoint templates that disobey this very guideline, leading many to think it's perfectly okay to put a lot of wimpy text on a busy background. Take this free template, for example:

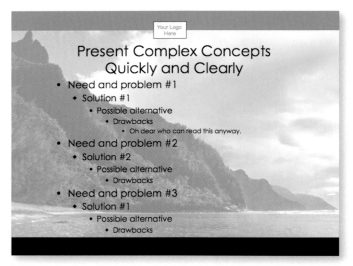

The text is directly on top of the distracting (and irrelevant) background; you assume that since Microsoft created it this way, it must be okay. Never assume that. This slide also gives you five levels of bullet points, as if anyone in the entire room could ever read past the second one. Heck, **you** can't even read past the second one. Use your own common sense. Microsoft is not the god of presentation design.

But the templates *are* getting better. If you have an old version of PowerPoint, it would behoove you to upgrade so you can get the new templates that are included with the application, and then download some new ones from the Microsoft site. Choose the templates with a consciousness about the purpose of your presentation; choose a background that supports your message.

The more complex the information, the simpler the background

Occasionally there is no way around the necessity of putting a lot of data on one slide. Just keep in mind that the more text, charts, graphs, or images that you *must* put on the slide, the simpler your background *must* be.

It's not necessary to have exactly the same background on every slide in your deck (see Chapter 8 for more on that topic), so if you've got a graphic theme you really like that ties your slides together, you can get away with eliminating parts that are not necessary when you have a lot of data on one slide.

It's not hard to find the irrelevant and unnecessary items on this slide (left). Make a habit of really *seeing* the individual elements so you can make decisions about what should go and what can stay.

When is a busy background okay?

A busy, complex background can be perfectly great if the data on that slide is large enough and bold enough to be understood—and if that background is relevant. See pages 110–113 for some great examples of using a busy background, but notice that you can still read the text! Why is that? Put it into words; the more often you clarify what works and what doesn't work and put it into words, the easier it is for you to automatically create better slides.

Don't use dorky clip art

You cannot use dorky clip art—especially dorky animation clip art—even if it comes with your software program. The days of using random clip art are over. Let go. There are a number of terrific places to get free or inexpensive professional-level illustrations and photographs (see page 154), or let your information stand on its own (with nice type).

Don't believe someone who tells you that you *must* have a graphic on every slide. That's baloney. And silly clip art on every slide only lowers the quality of your presentation.

The text on your page is the most important element. Images can be terrific and can add hugely to the emotional impact, but if their point is to add to the emotional impact, why use goofy pictures? Do they add to the clarity? Are they relevant? Probably not. Probably just the opposite. So be careful of the images you put on the page—make sure they *enhance* and *support* your text.

I'm really quite astounded by how many slideshows still use random and silly clip art on their slides, especially their already overcrowded slides.

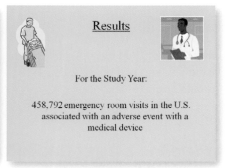

It's time to let go. The world has moved on from this type of graphic image and you need to catch up. Truly, no graphic at all is better than irrelevant and last-century clip art.

Maybe your piano recital group happens to be having its annual Brown Bag Martini luncheon and you found exactly what you need in PowerPoint's little collection. Okay.

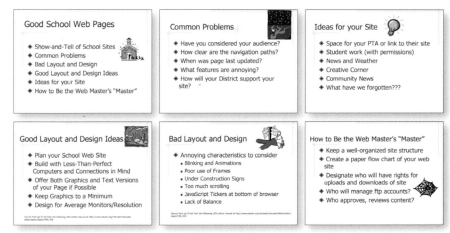

The arbitrary clip art on these slides is not relevant and it does not clarify the information. It adds visual interest, but not the positive kind.

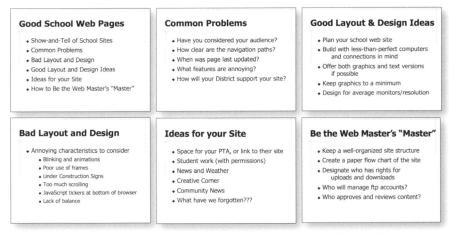

Really, it's **okay** to eliminate the clip art! These slides have enough visual interest without distracting little pictures. Without the clip art, you can make the headlines bolder (and a wee bit bigger). Also think about making those bullets smaller. *Emphasize what is important; tone back what is not.*

Remember, everything in and around the presentation reflects on you and impacts the perception of the value of what you're offering. If a picture is worth a thousand words, think of how much you'll have to say to make up for one goofy clip art image.

Use *relevant* photos

There is a trend in presentation design to use one full-screen graphic per slide. And the graphic has to be "high impact." I have seen a number of slideshows where the presenter followed that rule, but the high-impact graphics had nothing to do with the topic!

A problem with irrelevant images is that our minds are very visual so we are very attracted to the gorgeous or provocative photo. But our minds are also very practical, so they immediately start trying to place the photo into the context of the presentation topic. If there is no relevance, if the photo is completely random but gorgeous, our brains have to do a lot of processing to figure that out. Meanwhile you're talking away and I've missed half of what you said, gaping in awe at your high-impact photo with the right side of my brain and trying to use the left side of my brain to process what you're talking about at the same time.

If you choose to use high-impact photos as your design theme, you need to use them throughout the slideshow. The point is not to use one or two terrific photos and then put a dozen bullet points on the slides in-between—you need to commit to the design concept throughout the deck, or not. One option is to use a high-impact (and relevant) photo to introduce each topic. You introduce the topic with this mind-grabbing image to get the audience in the mood, then carry on with your beautifully designed text-based slides. Or use a slice of that photo as a repetitive element on the succeeding slides, as shown on page 90. Whatever you choose, make it relevant.

A problem with creating an entire slideshow with high-impact photos is that it can be difficult and time-consuming to get the perfect photo for each slide (assuming you're not using random, irrelevant images). Even if you can get the images inexpensively at iStockphoto.com, it's still time-consuming.

Video and animated clips

This also applies to video clips in your presentation (see the following chapter about the kinds of animation and transitions built within PowerPoint or Keynote). Don't be misled into thinking I want to watch some indiscriminate YouTube video as filler or mere entertainment—I'm using valuable time to come to your presentation to get specific information. Use video, by all means! But please make it worth my time. Be able to put into words why that particular video clip is relevant to your presentation. If you can, then use it!

5 Animation

Animation, of course, refers to things that move on the slide. **Transition** refers to the animation that can appear when one slide disappears and the next one appears.

I realize there are presentation gurus who insist that animation on slides is one of the greatest sins on earth. But the fact remains that we *like* a little animation. We *like* to spark things up a bit with moving parts. We *like* cool transitions.

And certain animations and transitions, respectfully implemented, can serve to clarify and enhance a presentation. *That's the key—respectful and relevant implementation.* Certainly there are millions of presentations that make your eyes cross because every single word comes flying in from around the corner, twirls in place, and slowly alights on the page. Again and again and again and again.

The problem with animations and transitions is not that they exist, but simply that they are misused. So in this chapter we'll look at ways to use these energetic features appropriately so they actually strengthen the communication rather than get in the way.

Animation creates a focus

This is the important principle to keep in mind: **animation creates a focal point.** So do not use it if it calls unwarranted attention to something, such as goofy clip art. Do not bring every piece of text swooshing in. Do not use the typewriter animation to make me sit through watching every one of your bullet points slowly type onto the screen. Please.

Use an animation or transition when you want to call attention to something.

Scarlett, Jimmy, Ryan

Scarlett & JohnD, Jimmy, Ryan

ActsOfGood.com web development

ForgedClothing.com · hard wear for hard people

I gave a talk to a Mac user group where they wanted to know my story. I used an Apple Keynote template and inserted photos of my kids when they were little, when I first started writing computer books. I copied that slide three times.

In the second slide, I replaced the baby photo of Scarlett with a current photo of Scarlett and her Sweet Heart. I used a dissolve transition so all that appeared to change on that slide was her face and the text. The dissolve focused on Scarlett.

In the third slide, I replaced Jimmy's face, and in the fourth slide, Ryan's. As each face changed, ***it became the focus because of the transition.***

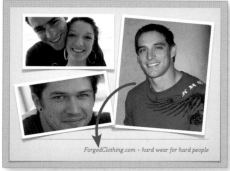

A problem that appeared in this sequence is that the text on each slide was ignored—when there's a human face to watch, that's what we watch.

I added a nice little text animation so after a few seconds of me talking about this child, the web address appeared in a little animation and **called attention to itself.** Appropriately.

While my kids were growing up, there were also lots of dogs in the house and they showed up in my books along with my kids. So I displayed a photo of the dogs (right).

Those dogs are all gone now, but I brought in a photo of the two we have now. After a couple of seconds of the original dogs, a nice little animation brought the two new dogs forward. Nothing obnoxious—it just easily refocused the audience's attention. And the animation I chose **reinforced the message** of these dogs entering our lives.

The old gang.

The old gang.

Pumpkin and Rosetta

Transitions and animations as complements

In this talk about various themes in *Macbeth,* I used transitions between and animations on every slide. They were carefully designed to be subtle and to complement the information, not to distract. Below are several sets of slides from the presentation.

This is a Keynote theme called Barcelona that I bought at KeynotePro.com. Using the various cube transitions in Keynote, I could make the red panel always lead to the next red panel around the edge of the cube so the transitions were predictable (less distracting) but still interesting.

Attendees had handouts that included all the lines we were going to talk about, so the slide presentation simply introduced each section.

As I'm talking (standing next to the screen), a spooky image relevant to the topic slowly appears in the space.

Occasionally a splat of blood appears on a slide, either quickly as if thrown, or slowly as if just appearing.

As I'm talking, a disembodied head slowly rises into the space.

When discussing the Porter who lets in the tailor to cook his goose, an antique tailor's goose (a pressing iron) moves into the screen, stops for a second, and moves off.

When discussing the prevalence of items in threes, a number 3 curls in around the side and in a moment gets spattered with blood.

After my "thank you" slide appears, it gets splotched with blood. Blood is a big motif in *Macbeth,* so to reinforce that imagery, it appears quite a bit in this presentation.

The blood splotches are from the "Supplemental Material" that is included with the Barcelona theme. They're actually ink blots, but I thought they worked quite well as blood.

Clearly transition between major topics

Slide transitions can be particularly useful as **visual cues** to signal transitions between major topics. I generally use a dissolve transition between most slides because I like its non-invasive feeling, but when I'm ready to move into another area, I use a transition that clearly cues the audience to what's happening.

For instance, after two or three intro slides, I often use a dramatic transition, like Keynote's doorway (shown below), into the body of the presentation. This alerts the audience that now we're getting down to business. When I use a dramatic transition this way, I stick to that same transition between other *major topics* (not between every slide) so the audience instantly understands its meaning; that is, I don't use every fancy possibility in the application.

The slide turns into a doorway to introduce the main presentation.

You can surely imagine how obnoxious it would be if every slide used such a dramatic transition.

Use transitions to keep your audience on track

Use *appropriate* but less dramatic transitions to guide your audience through the presentation. With conscientious thoughtfulness, you can use transitions to clue the audience as to when you are continuing in the same theme, making a shift in the topics, a segue, or a sharp turn.

These slides (using a template in Keynote) are a segment about the history of Shakespeare in America. Through this entire segment, slides unobtrusively dissolve from one to the next; the audience has no disruption in the flow of the talk. Until . . .

The slide above shoved to the *left* so it appeared to push the "Shakespeare, New Mexico" slide out of the way.

After a couple of seconds explaining "Sweet Swan Lane," a duplicate of "Shakespeare, New Mexico" shoved to the *right,* pushing "Sweet Swan Lane" out of the way, back to where it came from.

Visually, it clearly appeared that "Sweet Swan Lane" interrupted for just a few seconds and we immediately went back to the main presentation. The audience didn't have to worry that we were wandering down a new line of thought.

Use animation to illustrate and clarify

If animation can help to clarify an idea, by all means use it. In the example below, I wanted to show the six-mile route that a person in 1600 could use to get from Pembroke Castle, Wales, to Milford Haven. I could explain it easily, but it's much more memorable to see it in action.

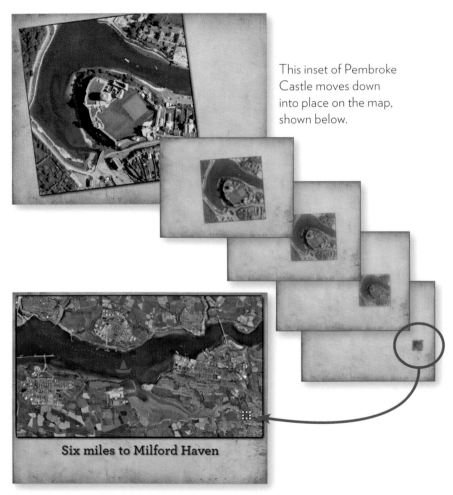

This inset of Pembroke Castle moves down into place on the map, shown below.

Six miles to Milford Haven

The "Magic Move" transition in Keynote let me take a close-up inset from a map and place it into context on the larger map.

Then I used the "Actions" palette to bring in a little boat that traveled the six miles by water to Milford Haven, along the dotted red line you see above (although the dotted line is not visible when the animation plays).

This was relevant animation that *clarified* my point in the talk and made it visually apparent, rather than just talking about the six-mile boat journey.

Animate a chart for clarity

Sometimes a chart or graph can benefit by a little animation to focus on a certain element. For instance, maybe you want to point out the rapid growth of a particular stock during a particular time period; you could show the chart with bars representing these stocks and animate that one bar/stock as it grows above the others. Or perhaps, in a pie chart, each piece pulls itself out from the pie as you discuss it.

Remember, your point with animation is to *clarify* with *relevant* focus. Don't just randomly make things twitch.

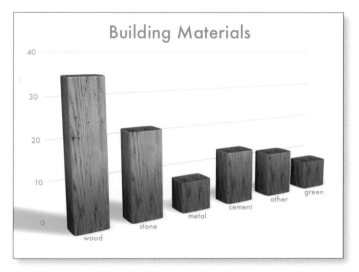

In this chart, each bar slowly rises at the moment you choose (click the mouse to make the next one appear), so you can talk about the important aspects of each building material individually before discussing them as a group.

The facts about animation

There are two important things to remember about transitions and animation.

One: **The movement calls attention to itself**, so only animate when you have something special that you want to call attention to.

When deciding whether or not to add animation to a slide, take a minute to put into words *why* you need to do that. If you cannot verbalize a good reason, let go. Don't do it.

For instance, does the silly clip art man doing cartwheels across the page clarify a point you're making? No? Get rid of him. But does a crowd scene that gets larger and larger *clarify* something in your presentation about population growth? Then by all means, have fun with it!

Two: **It's possible to use too much** animation and too many different and crazy transitions. Yes, by limiting them the audience doesn't get to see every amazing transition that your software has to offer, but too bad for them. They'll get over it. They might even thank you.

The power of animation and transitions is that it catches the eyes of the audience. As a presenter, you generally want most of the attention on you, so avoid a competing situation—when there is action on the slide, stop talking. Let the audience enjoy it for a second or two before getting back to business.

Plot

The plot of a presentation is its story line. A good plot has a beginning, a middle, and an end. As an audience, we like to be introduced to the presentation appropriately—we don't want to jump right into the middle. We want to know where we're going and what to expect. We want to travel an interesting road, not a boring, monotonous one. We want peaks and valleys, dangers and lulls; we want to be interested in the process. And when we've gotten to the end, we want to know we're there.

In a good film, the first five minutes (and often less) tells us what to expect; we know whether it's a thriller, romantic comedy, film noir, documentary, action/adventure, science fiction, etc. And this is important to us because our minds get emotionally prepared for what we are about to sit through.

And when the film/presentation starts winding down, we need to know that too. I'm sure you've seen movies that have two or three endings in a row—you think the zombie is dead and buried and the protagonists are safe when lo, up he pops out of the ground again. And again. It's really annoying.

Plot also involves the story itself, the connection to the human in us. As you're developing your talk, find ways to make visceral connections with your audience, if possible. You can do it with your visuals, your own manner of speaking, and the tale itself.

Make a beginning

Have you ever noticed that a published book has a half-title page (often), a copyright page, a full title page, a dedication page, an introduction, perhaps a preface, and sometimes even more pages before you finally get to the actual book? This is not just a process of legal notifications—it's the foreplay before you start reading. We enjoy that process.

A film works the same way—even if the film starts before the credits roll or it starts along with the credits, the first few minutes are still an introductory time, a setup, before we jump directly into the film. Think of your presentation in the same way.

I've seen too many slideshows where the first slide jumps right into the topic, sort of like opening a book and the very first page is Chapter One. Too often, the presenter has placed his introductory notes on the first page and reads them.

Think of your presentation as a story, even if you're telling the story of how to create a business plan or how to get divorced amicably or how to read Chaucer. Let the minds of the audience members move into your emotional space appropriately. You are much more likely to carry them along with you if you've set the scene and they know where you're going.

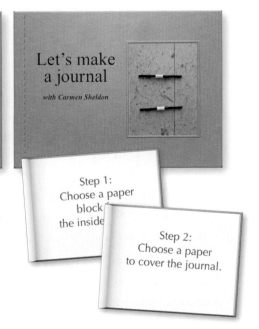

With this first slide, we jump right into the presentation. Remember, it doesn't cost any extra to make more slides. Give me an introduction, ease me into it.

In this Keynote template, one of the slides has a holding space for a graphic, so let's use that to show off a sample journal. Then walk me through it, one step/one slide at a time.

Tell us where you're going

After you give me an introduction to the general concept, spend a minute to describe where we're going. Whether it's a sales pitch, a teaching lesson, a moment in history, or a corporate overview, let me know where you plan to take me and even give me an idea of how long this will take. You can feel what happens inside yourself when I tell you this is going to take fifteen minutes, or if I tell you it's going to be two hours. I'm more likely to go with you for two hours if I *know* from the get-go to expect that. I'm even more willing if you give me a brief rundown of what we're going to see along the way.

Before launching directly into Step 1, I'd like an overview of the entire process so I know what to expect, how long it will take, am I gonna get dirty, what will I end up with?

Text vs. images

Not all presentations need images—many work perfectly well with simply text, especially if it's nice-looking text. And a few presentations work just fine using only images while the presenter talks.

Most of the time, however, we use a combination of both text and images. One way to think of the two of these working together is to consider the text on the slides as *the data;* the visual images as *the emotional impact.* You might be *telling* me the statistics on the number of women impacted by microcredit in a certain part of Africa, while you *show* me a woman in Magnambougou with her goat herd and children.

As you choose images to go with your presentation, keep in mind the difference between **data and emotion**; combine the two wisely.

Find the humans in the story

Whenever possible, try to show the human side of topics in your presentation. This is not so hard to do when you have ideas and charts and graphs that have to do with people; it's more difficult to do when you're teaching a class about NMR spectroscopy. So don't *force* a human story into a topic where it doesn't belong or where it might just complicate things, but if it does belong, take advantage of it.

For instance, do you have statistics about how many children go to kindergarten in Korea? Instead of just the dry data, find an image of Korean children going to school so we connect the human beings with the statistics. Try to include the *emotional* impact of a relevant image that embodies that *data*. But remember, don't add arbitrary or useless or confusing images just to create some random emotional moment.

Find the humans in the audience

Your manner of speaking, your manner of telling your presentation, can bring people into your talk or put them to sleep. You *must* talk to your audience. Look at them. Watch their faces for signs of boredom or enlightenment or confusion and respond accordingly.

In a Shakespearean play, it is most often the bad guy who talks directly to the audience in a soliloquy. Interestingly, this technique is what makes us love those bad guys in an odd way—Richard III, Edmund, Iago. Falstaff and Hamlet are not bad guys, but they have more soliloquies than any other characters in the canon and they are two of the most beloved of all. What Shakespeare knew is that by talking directly to the audience, we (the audience) develop a relationship with the speaker. Whether the speaker is a fat, cowardly realist or a ruthless murderer, we have a relationship and they bring us along with them. We want to go where they go and we want to follow them through their process.

Think of the storytelling you grew up with. Did your Grandma tell you a story and never include you in it, never look at you, never exclaim in wonder with you? Of course not. By drawing in your audience, you are more likely to get them on your side.

This can be true whether you are teaching the art of losing weight or of changing the world through green-energy automobiles or the quantitative analysis of molecular biophysics. Look at your audience, speak to them, listen to them—as one human to another—and they will come with you.

Tell *relevant* stories

We hear a lot about this idea of creating your presentation as a "story." Some people get a wee bit confused with this thought and think they should provide their entire presentation as a story or series of personal anecdotes.

One book I bought about giving presentations is told through the tale of two cavemen, an example of the idea of "story" taken to the extreme. To get the gist of the information I had to slog through silly baloney about cavemen creating presentations. "Oh Robin," you say, "Enjoy the process, go along for the ride, be in the moment." Personally, I would rather get to the point of what I need to know and save that precious time for talking to my kids, creating mosaic art, hiking across the desert. And then get back to work.

Yes, anecdotal true stories of the lives of people or animals or yourself can elucidate things—sometimes. Sometimes they just add unnecessary words and it's annoying. It seems to be a fine line.

Many, many presentations can benefit by uncovering the human interest. *But stories are not critical to every presentation.* Guy Kawasaki (GuyKawasaki. com) has a 10-20-30 rule for entrepreneurs who pitch to venture capitalists: 10 slides, 20 minutes, 30-point type. He wants straight talk.

If the story you want to tell is perfectly germane to the topic, *if* it moves the presentation forward, *if* it has an important life lesson that is integral to your subject, and *if* it's fascinating in some relevant way, go ahead and tell me. But be careful about making the presentation about *you.* I have seen presenters weave in their personal stories throughout an entire 60-minute presentation and what most of the audience comes away with is, "It's all about him."

Please understand that I am not denigrating the importance of story. I realize story is vitally important to the human race. When Prodigy did a study on how people used their Internet service after it had been out a year or two, they were surprised to discover that the overwhelming majority of people used it—not for business or trade or research—they used it to talk to each other, to listen to each other, to create relationships, to build stories.

I just encourage you to think long and hard about whether the personal stories you plan to include in your talk are about the information you are trying to communicate, or about *you.* Don't confuse the focus of your presentation by including *irrelevant* personal stories.

Vary the pace

Think of your favorite film and about how the pace varied throughout it: sometimes there's a fast onslaught of an exciting happening, then a restful pause, then some more stuff that isn't quite as exciting but it still moves the plot forward, then an intriguing slow moment, then a fast pace followed by another romantic pause. The story in your presentation can learn some lessons from films.

If you carry on through your presentation at the same pace, whether that pace is fast and furious or slow and thoughtful, it becomes monotonous. Consider how you can find some moments to breeze through half a dozen slides in thirty seconds, pause on one slide to discuss that topic for four minutes, show/discuss three slides in the next two minutes, stop on a slide for five minutes, open up a short discussion to the audience, etc. Vary your tone, move around, wave your arms, point your fingers, speak with authority and emotion. Remember that *you* are a human—don't become a mere appendage to the slide.

I would bet that your presentation automatically arranges itself in a varied pace—you just need to be conscious of that pace and work with it. Don't be afraid to show a few slides very quickly, even half a second per slide. In one of the screenwriting courses I've taken, the instructor showed a six-minute video clip of stills from hundreds of movies, shown for varying amounts of time. Some of the clips were only visible for *a quarter of a second.* The amazing thing was that our emotional minds *instantly* recognized the images—we knew who that was and which film, but our brains could not process it into *words* fast enough. It was kind of exhausting, not only because our pea-brains kept struggling to find the names and spew them out, but because each image evoked the entire movie, all the passion and hate and anxiety and tension and drama and love and humor. Images are so powerful.

So the point is that you can use explanatory imagery to skim through some parts of your presentation quickly—our minds absorb the images quickly enough. Slow down for other parts. Even words (in lowercase, not all capital letters) go into our brains instantly, so experiment with one or two words on slides that you skim through quickly. You'll find all kinds of ways to vary the pace—you just need to be aware of the concept and work with it.

Consider this portion of a talk I gave to graphic design teachers and students on the trend in design to use handmade elements. I was relating it to my own journey in doing things with my hands again and how those things you're interested in can lead to new ideas in your graphic design projects. The first six slides of this particular segment took about fifteen seconds, then we paused on the next two slides to talk about ways to incorporate images and text from old books into graphic design projects. (The template is from Keynote.)

"Several years ago I joined the Miniature Book Society and started collecting miniature books . . .

specifically miniature Shakespeare books . . .

from Europe that I had written in my early twenties into books for my kids . . .

specifically really crummy miniature Shakespeare books . . .

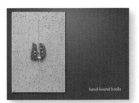

because I was also teaching myself the art of bookbinding to bind the 65 letters home . . .

and this process led to my collecting old, destroyed books whose pages can be used in a variety of ways in graphic design projects."

Make an end

Let the audience know when your presentation is over—don't let them have to awkwardly figure it out because you stopped talking. Just as a story has an ending, let your presentation have an ending. As an audience, we need to have that closure—it sets off a certain cue in our minds. You know that feeling at a play or performance when the lights go off and you're not sure if it's the end or just a scene change so you don't know whether or not to clap? We need the ". . . and they lived happily ever after" closing moment.

When you are close to the end, you might say something like, "I have one more point to make," or "Let me say this before I close," or "The final important thing to understand is . . . ." This sets us up, the audience, to tie it all together in our minds, get our questions ready, close our notebooks, and send one last tweet.

With a partner, look through a newspaper and find an example of an article that:

1. Informs
2. Entertains
3. Persuades
4. Serves

This is the last slide in a presentation for high school students about using the newspaper. Is it clear that this is the end? Not really—there's no clue whether or not another task follows this one.

Even if the instructor says, "And here is your last task," we still like a final opportunity to close the window. Give me a goodbye slide, please! End of story.

Then create a "Thank you" slide so there is no question that you are finished and they can applaud now. Or your slide might say, "Questions?" or "Applause Now" or "Thank goodness it's over" or anything else appropriate and *relevant*. Because it's your last slide and you haven't used much animation throughout your presentation (except where entirely relevant, right?), feel free to use your favorite gaudy transition to this goodbye slide (as shown on the opposite page). It might wake up your audience.

Saying goodbye and thank you is the perfect time to use the most obnoxious transitions in your collection.

And leave time for questions

An audience, as you well know because you've been in an audience many a time, always appreciates the *opportunity* to ask questions at the end of a presentation, whether or not they actually ask any. I spent two days at a seminar given by a very famous communications guru who not only hated any sort of visual presentation so I don't even remember nine-tenths of what he talked about (I don't retain much of what goes in my ears), but he also refused to answer questions from the group. It made me feel like he was hiding something, like he didn't want to be put on the spot about anything, sort of like the people who demo software at trade shows but refer all questions to the other people who actually know what they're talking about.

So stand up and be honest—ask for questions. If you can't field questions about your subject, you shouldn't be talking about it. You might be in a situation where someone can catch tweets or other online questions for you; this is a great resource for people who are too shy to stand up in a crowd and ask. Obviously, there are some presentation situations where questions are not part of the program, but if it's expected, rise to the occasion. If you ask for questions and there are none after about six seconds, say, "Thank you very much," and leave the stage to thunderous applause.

The worst presentation I've ever attended (well, one of the worst)

I was taking a summer Shakespeare program at Oxford University a couple of years ago. I attended an extracurricular presentation on the architecture of Oxford. The room was hot and stuffy, dark, the chairs were packed together, and the audience was mostly seniors (as in older people, not college seniors).

The professor used the old-fashioned slides and carousel that he'd been using for a hundred years. He sat in a chair in the audience about five rows back, on the aisle, facing the screen, and clicked his carousel. No one could see him, nor could he see his audience. Thus we heard this disembodied voice in the dark drone on about surprisingly boring things as we looked at faded slides. And thus the professor had no idea that by halfway through his talk, eighty percent of his audience in that warm, stuffy room were quietly snoring away.

FOUR
principles of
VISUAL
PRESENTATION
Design

DESIGN THE SLIDES

Now that you've got your presentation organized, your text is crisp and crystal clear, you've got an idea of relevant graphics and backgrounds you'd like to use, you understand where you might want to use animation appropriately, and you've figured out the plot of your presentation story, you're ready to actually design it.

This section reiterates the four basic design principles I first codified in *The Non-Designer's Design Book* and shows you how they apply to presentation design.

Four principles of **visual** presentation design

The four principles of design that I first codified and explained in *The Non-Designer's Design Book* apply equally well to presentation slides. It's quite amazing how these four little concepts can so easily transform an amateur look to a professional one. Each one is explained more fully in the following pages. Then we'll work with applying all of these principles to a presentation.

Contrast

If two items are not exactly the same, make them different. Really different. Contrast intrigues us because it creates an interest, often it creates a focal point. Contrast is drama, but it's also a tool for organizing the information on your slides.

Repetition

Repeat some aspect of the design throughout the entire piece. Repeating elements throughout a slideshow is what unifies your entire presentation. This doesn't mean everything has to look the *same*—you just need graphic elements that tie everything together.

Alignment

Nothing should be placed on the slide arbitrarily. Every item should have at least one edge connected to something else on the page.

Proximity

Group related items together; physical closeness implies a relationship. Information *groups* help clarify what's on the screen.

Keep in mind that the point of *designing* your presentation (as opposed to putting things on the slides without thinking about its visual presentation) is not just to make it pretty—**the point is to communicate more clearly.** These design principles not only make it look better, but along the way the information will be presented more coherently, simply, and straightforwardly.

And it is just a fact that if your presentation is visually pleasing, people are more likely to look at your slides instead of their text messages.

Contrast

Contrast is probably the single most important feature of design that makes things appealing to our eyes. Glancing at the two slides below, both of which say exactly the same thing, to which one do you feel your eyes pulling toward?

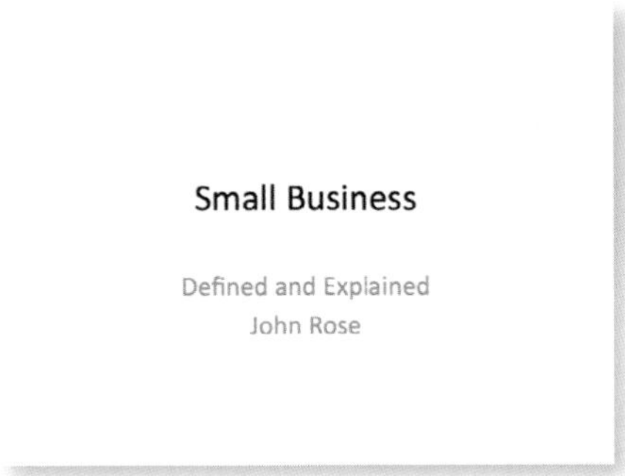

Small Business

Defined and Explained
John Rose

Small Business

Defined and Explained
John Rose

This is PowerPoint's default slide opener. There's not much contrast on this page—the text is practically all the same size; the colors are similar; the white page is more important than the black type; it's all rather wimpy. If you show this as your opening slide, you look wimpy. Tidy, but wimpy.

With a contrast in the size of the type and the strong black/white, your eyes are pulled into this slide. And it gives you, the presenter, a more substantial impact.

Contrast with typeface

You can create contrast in all sorts of ways. One of the easiest is by using a strong typeface. Remember, sometimes people are in the back of a large room, so not only does contrast make the slide stronger, it makes it easier to read. Clarity!

These slides are nice and clean, but they have no impact. In fact, the "Proposal Contents" slide is downright impossible to read. (If it's small on your computer screen, it's going to be small in the lecture room as well.)

Now we not only see what's on the screen, but the stronger impact has a subtle effect on me (in the audience) in that I feel more confident in what I see.

Notice the "Proposal Contents" slide no longer has all those tiny bullet points; those points have been expanded into further slides and this one is now just the overview of what's coming up.

Notice also that the actual bullets are gone. Can the clutter.

Small black text on a big white slide is wimpy; it's fine in print, but not on a slide. And only people in the first two rows can read it!

I realize the first set of slides below uses the default slide theme in PowerPoint, but you don't have to use that template. At least enlarge your type size as a simple contrast. And remember, it's easier to enlarge the text if you have less of it. Edit!

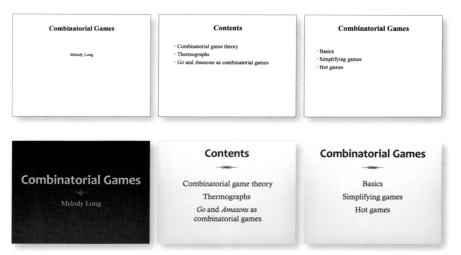

This example uses a template in PowerPoint, but I did have to make the type larger than its default point size. Notice this type isn't a huge size—it's simply a more readable size. Contrast doesn't have to be extreme to be effective.

Contrast with color

You can create contrast with the colors on your slides. I'm actually quite surprised by the number of slides I've seen that look like the two directly below. Really truly honestly, can you create that slide on your computer and sincerely say that it's easy to read? Keep in mind that on your monitor, the light comes from behind and glows *through* the glass straight to your eyes; on a presentation screen, the light *reflects off* the screen and bounces back to your eyes, so the contrast of colors is even weaker.

Always remember that no matter how great it looks on your computer, it's not going to be that bright and that clear on a projector screen; it might not even be the same color. This is especially true if you like to present with the lights on.

If you have any doubt at all about your text being difficult to read on a projection screen, change it. "When in doubt, don't." (That's another of the Rules of Life.)

So much about design is really about *seeing*. Since you are reading this book, I assume you are interested in seeing more clearly—all it takes is a conscious effort. Be aware of what you see. **Listen to your eyes.**

The problem with the slides above is that there is not enough **contrast** between the background and the text. And it's not just the colors, but the busy backgrounds don't contrast with the wimpy type. If you really want this background, *then contrast the type,* as shown on the opposite page.

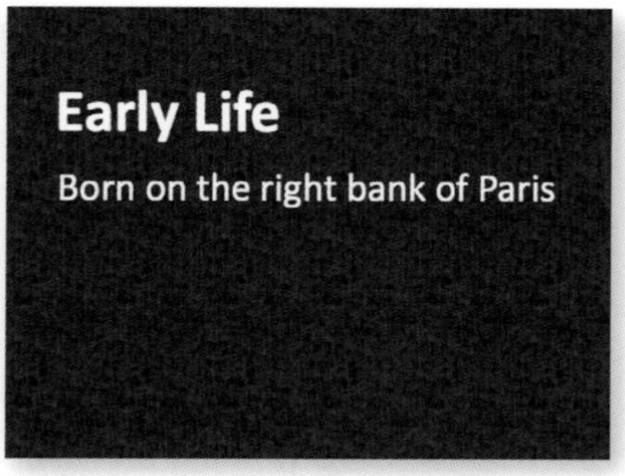

Marcel Proust
his life and work

Early Life
Born on the right bank of Paris

It's much easier to contrast the type and the background, of course, when there is less text. Edit. Open up those slides. Use as many as you need.

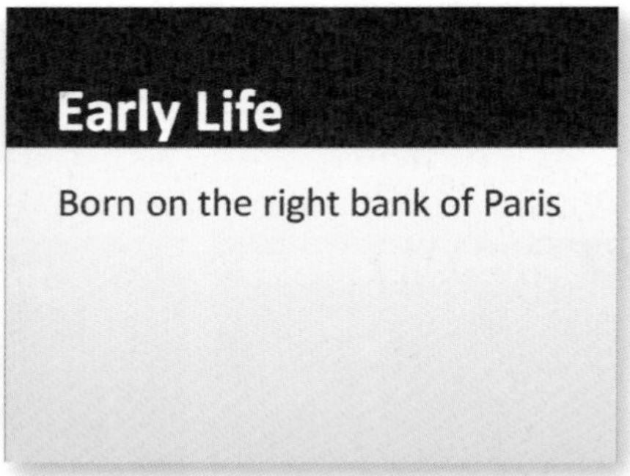

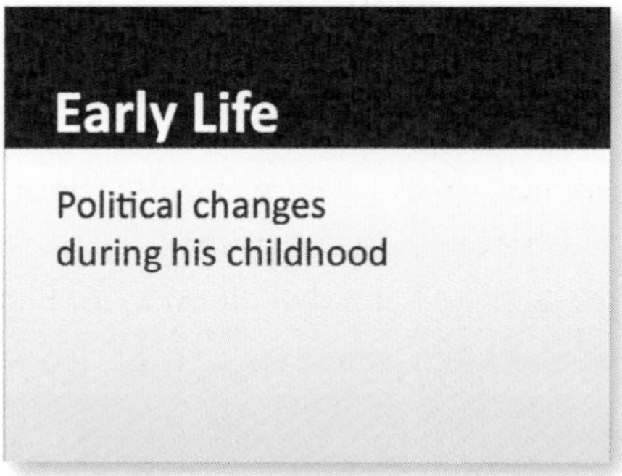

Marcel Proust
his life and work

Early Life
Born on the right bank of Paris

You can carry a piece of that busy background into the other slides as a unifying element, as shown here. This is the principle of repetition, as you'll see in the next chapter. It lets you use your favorite busy background in a suitable way.

Early Life
Political changes
during his childhood

Contrast provides substance

Contrast can provide a solid foundation from which to deliver your talk. Slides that use strong contrast tend to look substantial, and when you are confident in the vigorous foundation of your slides, that can translate to increased confidence for you as you present.

Wimpy. Sorry, but these are just wimpy slides. Why are the images so small? Why is the text so cowardly? Please don't make me use binoculars!

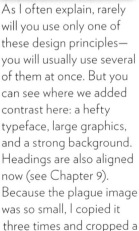

As I often explain, rarely will you use only one of these design principles— you will usually use several of them at once. But you can see where we added contrast here: a hefty typeface, large graphics, and a strong background. Headings are also aligned now (see Chapter 9). Because the plague image was so small, I copied it three times and cropped a different segment from each one, allowing me to enlarge it; as the slides dissolve one into the other, all that appears to change on each slide is the graphic. Now the audience can actually see the graphics.

Use contrast to organize

Contrast between elements creates an organization. The contrast on each slide helps to guide the viewer's eyes through the information because our eyes are attracted to the oppositions. On most slides, of course, there isn't a lot of information on each one (well, there shouldn't be) to worry too much about its organization, but you will run across instances when this will be important and it's good to know how to manage it.

The hierarchy you set up through contrast can become a repetitive element (see the following chapter) that helps your audience follow along with you.

College Procedures: How and Where to Apply	College Procedures: Skills Assessment

This presenter has a good start with contrast; she's pulling out important statements with a contrast of color. But she could emphasize it a little more. (And she could edit the text on the slides so there's not so much on each one.)

She strengthened the contrast in the headings: "College Procedures" is smaller, the unnecessary colon is gone, and the main heading is larger and bolder to attact our eyes.

She spread out the text onto more slides (note how "Skills Assessment" has opened up) so the information is large enough to read, then used the gold color for the most important info. The contrast pulls our eyes toward it.

Contrast demands attention

By its very nature, contrast calls attention to itself. You have surely been (or can imagine being) in a place where the way you look is very different from all those around you—even though you may be a very ordinary person amongst your own kind, you stand out in some places by contrast. It's pretty much the same in a slideshow, so take advantage of that. For instance, perhaps you are going along talking, talking, talking, showing your slides, and there's something coming up that is so stunning that you really want your audience to sit up and take notice—give it a remarkable contrast.

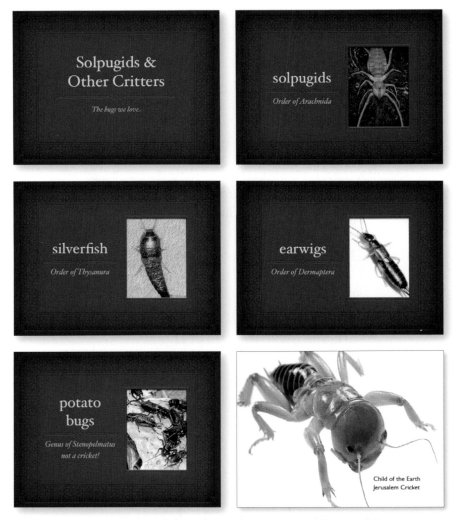

You can imagine sitting in a darkened room looking at small bugs and then—kapow—the most Magnificent Insect of All appears on the screen, hugely.

Repetition

Repetition is a feature that unifies a designed piece, especially when there are multiple parts, such as lots of slides in a presentation.

Repetition in its simplest form is consistency—you want to create a consistent look throughout your presentation. You might repeat the font choice and size; perhaps there are certain colors you can repeat; you might have graphic styles, placement of items, the arrangement of text and graphics, etc. Anything that appears more than once in your collection of slides, you can use as a repetitive element.

Most of the time you'll be working with the existing items on your slides, but sometimes you can *create* repetitive items specifically as unifying design elements. For instance, perhaps your talk is about astronomy and you have a particular star symbol you use in your introduction; you might use that star symbol as a repetitive element (in various sizes and colors, even) on slides here and there throughout your deck.

Repetition creates a consistent look

The simplest use of repetition is to create a consistent look throughout your deck of slides. This doesn't mean that every slide looks exactly the same; it just means that you are conscious of creating a collection that looks like everything belongs together.

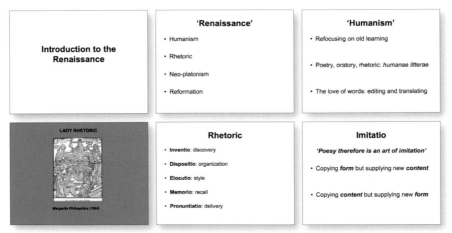

In these slides (six out of thirty-seven), the font and the white background might be considered repetitive elements, except they have no character. And there are several inconsistencies that are not intentional: the sizes of the fonts, the spaces between the lines, the positions of the text, the one slide with a dull gray background.

First of all, we'll just do one thing: Instead of using the default background, let's *intentionally* give it a *relevant* background. (I changed the font on this intro slide in Chapter 4.)

INTRODUCTION TO THE

RENAISSANCE

LYNN ROBSON, PH.D.

INTRODUCTION TO THE

RENAISSANCE

Humanism
Rhetoric
Neo-platonism
Reformation

HUMANISM

- Refocusing on old learning
- Poetry, oratory, rhetoric: *humanae litterae*
- The love of words: editing and translating

HUMANISM

Lady Rhetoric

Margarita Philosophica 1504

RHETORIC

- **Inventio**: discovery
- **Dispositio**: organization
- **Elocutio**: style
- **Memoria**: recall
- **Pronuntiatio**: delivery

RHETORIC IMITATIO

'Poesy therefore is an art of imitation'

- Copying *form*
  but supplying new *content*
- Copying *content*
  but supplying new *form*

Here we're starting to develop some repetitive design elements (some consistency) using the fonts, the spacing, the alignments.

This slide deck contains 37 slides so there will be constant adjustments as I go through it, working to create repetitive and consistent elements.

HUMANISM

- Refocusing on old learning
- Poetry, oratory, rhetoric: *humanae litterae*
- The love of words: editing and translating

HUMANISM

Lady Rhetoric

Margarita Philosophica 1504

RHETORIC

- **Inventio**: discovery
- **Dispositio**: organization
- **Elocutio**: style
- **Memoria**: recall
- **Pronuntiatio**: delivery

RHETORIC IMITATIO

Poesy therefore is an art of imitation

- Copying *form*
  but supplying new *content*
- Copying *content*
  but supplying new *form*

You read the previous chapter on Contrast, so you can see how I added contrast as a repetitive element.

Not only is this more compelling to look at, but can you see how it is also shaping up to communicate more clearly? The different sections are more apparent now.

To ensure that attendees notice when the main head changes, I might add a *subtle* animation to the new heading the first time it appears to call attention to it.

Repeat a style

Let's redesign these three slides with the ideas of both contrast and repetition in mind. Because the topic of games is so visual, let's use inexpensive photos from a site such as iStockphoto.com.

But first, let's edit: What *needs* to be on the slides, what will I be speaking *aloud,* and what will be on the *handout* that the audience takes home? I'm thinking the only thing that needs to be on each of these slides is the headline. I will talk about the other points, plus they have a handout with my outline to follow along with and write notes on. When I need to elaborate on one or more of the bullet points, I'll create more slides (as shown on page 90).

Let's start with an introductory slide that's on the screen while you're being introduced and while you make your introductory remarks (see Chapter 6 on Plot).

Each slide unobtrusively dissolves into the next.

The text that's on the original slide (top left) is the text you will be speaking, so you don't want it on the slide! The key points that you want your audience to remember are on the handouts.

Strong visuals of games and humans reinforce your talk without distracting from it.

That might look like a huge switcheroo, going from the original slides to the finished product. But it isn't, really. You just have to make a commitment to 1) edit the text so only what is really necessary is on the slide (remember, your slides are designed to *augment* your talk), and 2) invest a couple of dollars in images that reinforce your presentation.* Collecting fonts helps too.

In this example, I used a font I bought for $39 from MyFonts.com (it's Profumo, not Arial or Times). I added the dark horizontal bars and large photos. Each of these elements (font, bar, photo) acts as a repetitive element. By making the headlines graphically interesting, they become elements that act as repetitive, unifying features. And by using the photographs in a similar way, they also become repetitive, unifying elements. Notice I didn't use a photo here and silly clip art there, but maintained a consistent style.

Well, you might say, the original slides also have repetitive type treatments and a repetitive use of clip art. And you're absolutely correct. The difference is that the repetition on the original slides is weak; it's not conscious or consistent or even nice-looking. And the three graphic images have no consistency in style, color, or placement. There is nothing binding those three graphics together except that they were all randomly thrown onto the page.

Our minds really like organization. As I'm sitting in a presentation and listening to the speaker, my mind wants to be interrupted as little as possible. With consistent and repetitive (and relevant) elements in a slideshow, I feel calm and safe and it gives me a little more trust in the presenter. Do we judge a book by its cover? Of course we do, and we unconsciously judge a presentation by the way it looks and the way it makes us feel while we're watching and listening. We are a visual society.

*To find these images, I went to iStockphoto.com and searched for *board games* and *solitaire* and *video games,* separately. There were hundreds of images to choose from. It took ten minutes and cost $12.

Repeat the image, but differently

Repetition doesn't mean repeating *exactly* the same thing every time. You can repeat the same style of imagery, the same color, the same placement, anything that creates a repetitive pattern to unify the slides. Below, to expand on the topic of "What is a Game?," I might use a small piece of the original graphic in those individual slides. This helps the audience follow along with me; it creates not only unity but clarity.

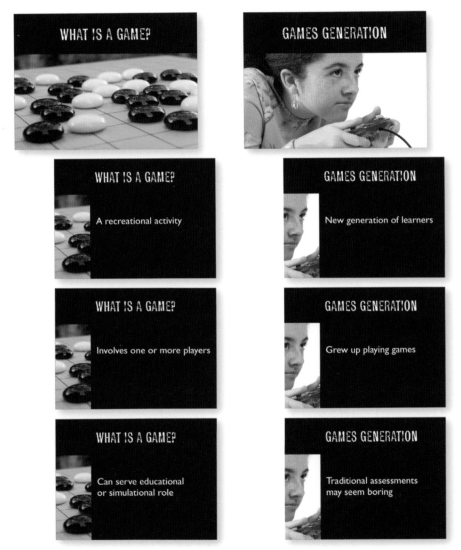

Use a dissolve transition with slides like these so the audience doesn't have to watch the heading and photo redraw on every screen; the only item that *appears* to change is the bullet point.

Unity with variety

If an element has a strong visual appeal, you can repeat it in different ways and still provide unity. Or if you have elements that are obviously part of a set (geometric figures, perhaps), you can use them in a variety of ways. Perhaps you have a circle motif going on—the circle is such a strong shape that you can use it in various sizes and colors and placements, and it still creates a unified look. Perhaps you have photos of houses as a theme—use all different sorts of houses. The stronger your repetitive elements are, the greater you can vary them and still maintain a consistent look and feel.

If your visuals are strong images, you can use them in a huge variety of ways—big, small, different colors, different placements, with different fonts, etc. (These sticky notes are from iStockphoto.com.)

These intro and overview slides set up a style from which the presenter can deviate in many ways and still maintain consistency.

Within this simple, repetitive framework, you can move the black bar, change the graphics, even change the colors (always with an aim to provide clarity)

91

Find repetitive elements and design them

Find the items in your presentation that are already repetitive, then use those items as design elements. Do you have a series of quotes? Perhaps oversized quote marks can become a repetitive element that calls attention to the clever remark. Do you have a phrase you keep coming back to? Perhaps a special type treatment for it can become a repetitive element.

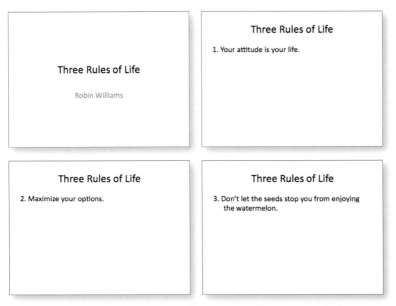

This short presentation uses the default slides in PowerPoint. At least the font is nice—this Calibri is much cleaner and fresher than Arial.

Generally, you don't want to focus on the numbers in a numbered list because you would call too much attention to them. But in this case, the number is part of the point, so let's make it a repetitive design element. (And let's add some contrast in the process.)

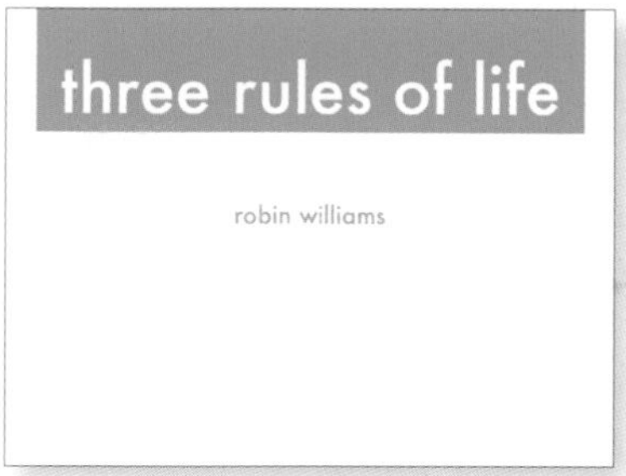

three rules of life

robin williams

This is based on a template in Keynote that I tweaked a bit.

The number 1 slide (below, left) dissolves into the next slide (to the right) where the number itself fades back and the rule is highlighted. Thus the numbers become a design element.

1

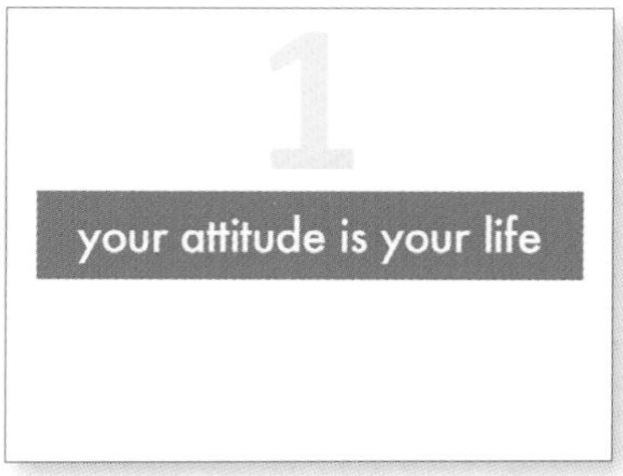

1

your attitude is your life

2

2

maximize your options

3

3

don't let the seeds stop you from enjoying the watermelon

thank you

The color of this last slide is different from the others, but the shape of the box, the font, the color of the font, and the placement are all repetitive. When you have a strong repetition, you can break out of it and it looks purposeful rather than like a mistake.

Repetition doesn't mean sameness

The principle of repetition doesn't mean *everything* is the same. You can easily have several different backgrounds, different fonts, different colors, different styles, etc., in the same deck of slides. The point to remember is that *repetition is a unifying element*. If you have a strong theme running through your slides, you can break out of it to focus on a new topic or a sideline, then return to your main look. Or use a variation of your main theme for sub-topics.

Repetition helps the audience keep track of what you're doing without having to think about it; it provides a solid visual ground upon which to base your presentation; it makes the audience feel safe and taken care of; it makes you look organized and sure of yourself.

However, repeating your company logo on every slide is NOT an example of repetition—it's an example of unnecessary and annoying clutter. See page 47.

This is the Light Table view in Keynote (use the Slide Sorter view in PowerPoint), with my slides for a talk on the Humours. You can see the repetitive elements throughout the entire deck, as well as for individual segments on each of the four humours. Each variation in the repetitive look was designed to augment the communication and understanding.

Alignment

Alignment organizes the various elements on your page and presents a structured and coherent look. It cleans up the page and helps to communicate more clearly.

The concept of alignment calls for conscious decisions about where you place items on the page. Don't ever stick something on the page in some random spot! Every item needs to be connected to something else on that individual slide, and your collection of slides should have consistent alignments throughout the deck. No more sticking things in empty corners—make sure elements are aligned.

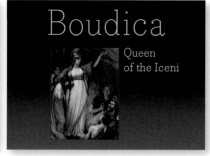

The items on this slide have no connection to each other—each one is just tossed onto the page randomly.

If we just do one thing—align each item with something else—see how the slide is instantly more organized.

The photo is aligned on the left edge of the heading, with the vertical bar of the B. The smaller text is aligned with the top of the photo and is now flush left so its left edge aligns with the edge of the photo.

Alignment cleans up individual slides

Even if you have a lot of text on your slide (not recommended but sometimes you might feel it's necessary), alignment is the most important tool you have to make all that potential busyness appear calm and collected.

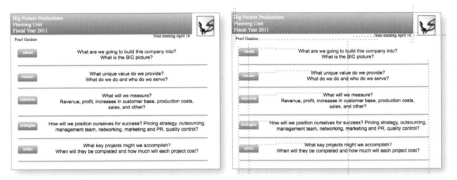

If you take a pencil and draw lines along all the edges of shapes and text boxes, or through the centers of center-aligned text, you see a lot of lines. That's what's making it look so messy.

But if we just align the objects, it's amazing how it cleans up the look. And a clean slide is a more communicative slide.

I changed those small blue boxes to match (repeat) the shape of the bar across the top; getting rid of those fussy corners on the small shapes helps tidy up the slide.

You can see that every item on the page is now aligned with something else.

Yes, the slide still has too much text (which makes it too small to read) but at least it is clean and organized, which helps immensely.

It's really quite remarkable how this one quick and easy thing can make such a radical difference in your slides.

There isn't much tying all these slides together; everything is sort of haphazardly placed on the slides.

Now there are several alignments on the individual slides and across the slides. In the middle one, the three lines of type forced the two photos down, but that's okay because there is still alignment across the headlines and between the two photos. Notice that *everything* doesn't have to be lined up (not *both* top and bottom, for instance); you just need some consistent connections.

But let's do one thing more—let's use more slides. They're free! These images are terrific and very emotional. With a dissolve transition between slides in each set, the text will appear to stay in the same place and just the photos will change. You create a much greater impact because your audience can actually see the photos.

Alignment cleans up your deck of slides

In a collection of slides, alignment not only makes individual slides cleaner and more organized, it makes your entire presentation cleaner and more organized as you repeat the alignments throughout the deck.

The elements on these slides were thrown on the page with no thought to their placement. The look is chaotic. (The excessive red doesn't help. And get rid of lengthy and complex web addresses that no one can read or write down; if it's important, put it in the handout.)

Now there are consistent alignments. You can practically see the invisible line running under all the headlines. The smaller text is aligned flush left, and that strong flush left is aligned against the strong edge of the portraits. The portraits themselves are now all the same size and aligned with each other as the slides progress. (These public domain images were free from Wikimedia Commons at commons.wikimedia.org.)

While we're looking at these slides, I just want to say something about the current trend of solid black backgrounds: Try something else. Perhaps solid black really is what you need for your presentation, or you like the way your slide bleeds into the background when it's projected, but at least try other colors. There are lots of rich, dark colors to choose from in this world. Or maybe it doesn't need to be dark! Lighten up!

Alignment unifies your deck

The example below is the same one I showed in the previous chapter where I applied repetition. But alignment is also a big factor in this example (rarely will you use just one of these design principles in any project). You can see that creating guidelines to align items across slides can unify an entire collection.

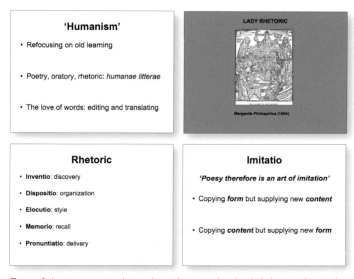

Few of the items are aligned on these individual slides or throughout the collection of slides.

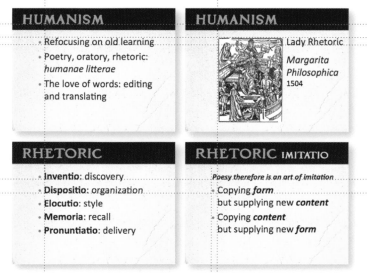

If you draw lines between the items on the individual slides, you see they are now more unified by alignment.

Alignment makes you look smarter

It's true. You are your slides. If they are sloppy and unclear, it naturally follows (in many minds) that you are sloppy and unclear or that your information is not sound. It's not a conscious decision on the part of the audience—it just happens. So look smarter and be smarter. Align those objects!

Again, you can see that not one of these five items on the slide has any relationship with any other item. (And the text is rather small.)

Now you can draw lines between items and see how they are connected. You can also see that I cropped the image of Iago so I could make him larger.

Let's also see how it looks without a black background. Hmm, seems a little easier to read. (Dark text on a light background is always easier to read.)

Bad men in Shakespeare

Richard III   Iago

images are from commons.WikiMedia.org

Alignment is a great organizer

Alignment is the single most important guideline to follow to visually organize the material on your slides.

I hope you are starting to **see** how nothing is aligned or connected to anything else on these slides—it's all a random hodgepodge.

Personally, I would get rid of this background, but the presenter apparently really likes it. So let's work with it instead of piling stuff on it willy-nilly; let's keep items inside the boundaries created by the background.

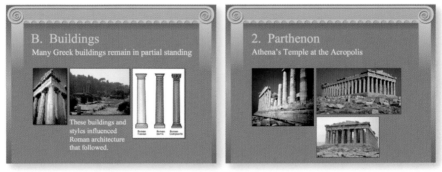

Now everything is aligned with something else. Take a moment to draw the alignments with a pencil, both on the individual slides and across both slides.

I deleted the single bullet graphic on each page. If there's only one bullet, what's the point?

I gave all the images the same 1-point border (repetition). (I also reduced the sizes of the images that were too low-res to be displayed so large.)

There is now the same amount of space between the graphics on all slides (repetition and alignment).

Break the alignment—intentionally

When developing your presentation, you'll probably find that you need to adjust your alignments as you go along in order to keep them consistent across slides. Learn to use your software to set up your own master page that suits your material. If you're using PowerPoint, it often makes up its own mind about the sizes of fonts and the placement, so I remind you once again to learn your software, learn how to control PowerPoint—don't let it control you (see Chapter 12 for some tips).

Sometimes you will have a few slides that can't fit into the alignment you set up, and that's okay. If you have a strong alignment across the slides, then when you *intentionally* break out of that alignment it will *look* intentional instead of random and chaotic. Now, this doesn't give you license to arbitrarily ignore how you place items on the slide—you must be able to put into words exactly why you decided to break the alignment for that particular slide and why it's okay.

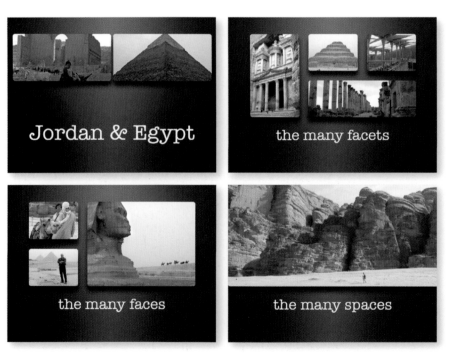

So you're going along and all your graphics are neatly fitting into certain spaces you have designated when, lo and behold, you really want to do something different with this one. That's perfectly great! As long as you've got a solid foundation holding your deck together, you can break out of it with glee.

Proximity

Whether or not various items on the slide are in close proximity or not instantly tells the viewer whether or not those items are related. The spaces between elements are critical to our immediate understanding.

The closer together elements are *physically,* the closer they seem *intellectually.* As the elements move farther apart, they separate themselves intellectually. Keep that in mind as you arrange items on the slide.

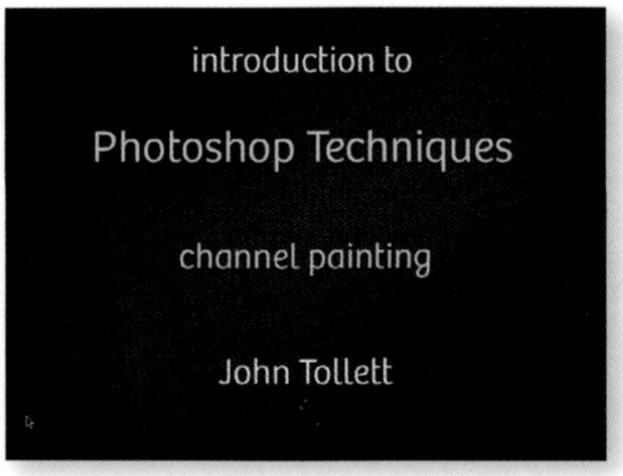

introduction to

Photoshop Techniques

channel painting

John Tollett

introduction to
Photoshop Techniques
channel painting

John Tollett

How many individual elements are on this slide? With all that space between each line, it looks like four separate and unrelated pieces of information.

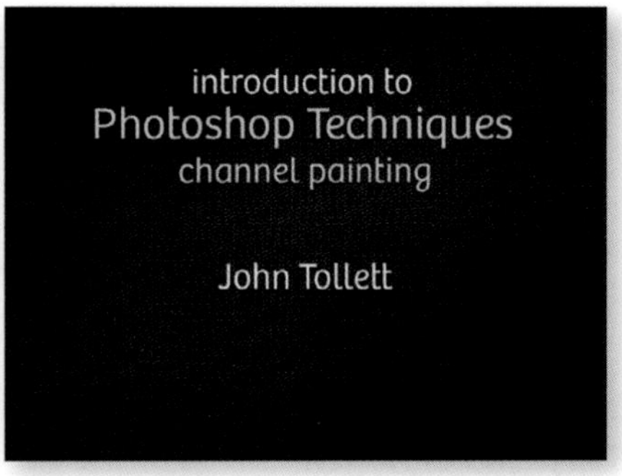

By simply grouping the items into closer proximity, we reduce the number of individual elements on this small slide from four to two.

And we can instantly see, even if this were in a foreign language, that we have a topic and a byline.

Create relationships

Proximity creates relationships. We automatically assume that items that are close together have connections, so be conscious of this on your slides. Think of human beings and how we make assumptions on their relationships based on their proximity (or not) to each other; next time you are in a group of people, consciously notice who has a relationship with whom, and why do you think that? Apply that thought to the pieces of information on your slide—who has relationships?

Combine proximity with alignment and you can't go wrong. Your slides will not only look nicer, but your information will be presented more clearly.

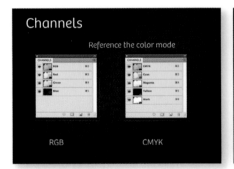

The subhead, above, is closer to the graphics than it is to the heading. And the captions, RGB and CMYK, are farther away than they should be.

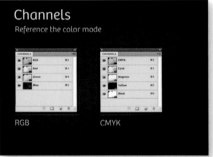

Simply by paying attention to the proximity of the elements (and their alignments), this slide is organized and communicates quickly and easily.

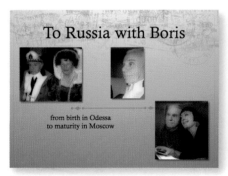

Don't just randomly throw things on the slide! Group elements together that belong together.

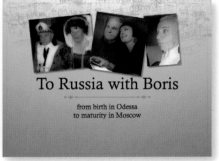

Now your eyes don't have to wander all over the page trying to make sure you've caught everything.

Do you also see the alignment used on this slide? (Centered.)

White space is okay

Sometimes presenters try to spread out the text to fill the empty space. You don't need to do that. It's okay to have empty space, or "white" space. In fact, one key feature of professional graphic design is *organized* white space; that is, the white space is as consciously placed as the individual elements.

You don't need to worry about where your white space is—*it will be organized and where it belongs if you follow the four basic principles.* Notice the white space in the examples below. You can see that when we apply the principle of proximity, that very process organizes the white space as well, without even thinking about it. What *you* have to do is let the empty space be there.

Next Steps

❖ Complete systems analysis by Aug. 31

❖ Install financial analysis system by Oct. 15

❖ Complete staff training by Nov. 20

❖ Begin transition to new system by Jan. 1

Next Steps

❖ Complete systems analysis by Aug. 31
❖ Install financial analysis system by Oct. 15
❖ Complete staff training by Nov. 20
❖ Begin transition to new system by Jan. 1

Can you see the empty space? Do you see how it's forcing the separate elements apart? Even the bullets are too far away from their lines of text.

Now the white space is organized, but you didn't have to do anything— it organized itself when you grouped elements into closer proximity.

Next Steps

❖ Complete systems analysis by Aug. 31

❖ Install financial analysis system by Oct. 15

❖ Complete staff training by Nov. 20

❖ Begin transition to new system by Jan. 1

Next Steps

❖ Complete systems analysis by Aug. 31
❖ Install financial analysis system by Oct. 15
❖ Complete staff training by Nov. 20
❖ Begin transition to new system by Jan. 1

I realize that when using a template in PowerPoint, it can automatically spread out the information like this. That's why you have to learn how to use your software; learn how to make it do what YOU want it to do (see Chapter 12).

It's okay to have lots of white space on the slide. You don't have to try to fill the white space by spreading out the text (that doesn't work, anyway).

But avoid *trapped* white space

When you combine proximity with alignment, you can ensure that you don't have "trapped" white space, or space that is enclosed between two objects. White space needs to flow, needs to have an outlet. When you trap it, the space forces those objects apart, as you saw on the previous page.

A very common design situation is the one shown below, where you have text and a photograph together, side by side. The photograph has a strong alignment—both of its edges are straight and definite. The text (unless it's centered) has a strong alignment on *one* of its edges, the edge against which it is aligned (typically, most text is lined up on the left side).

If you *combine* the strengths, *combine* the alignments—align the strong part of each object with the strong part of the other—you can do two things at once: eliminate any trapped white space, and add strength to your layout.

Above, the photographs have vertical lines, strong and straight. The text, being flush left, has a strong alignment on the left. The varied alignment on the right of the text creates "trapped" space between the text and the photo, pushing them apart.

If we align the strong lines (align the straight edge of the text along the straight edge of the photograph), it gives the white space room to flow off the page. And our design is strengthened because we've created groupings of information instead of having floating, random pieces.

Proximity cleans and organizes

Moving elements into appropriate groups immediately cleans up the slide and helps organize your information.

Always be conscious of how many times your eye must jump from one thing to another on a slide. In the example below, on the left, note your eye movements as you look at the slide. When you've looked at all five elements, can you feel your eyes still wandering around, trying to ensure you've seen everything? And can you imagine doing that while someone is talking and you need to take notes?

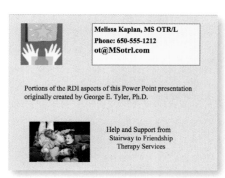

How many elements are on this small slide? Do any of them *look* related to any other? Intellectually, are there items that *should be* more closely connected?

Obviously, I did a lot more than just group items into closer proximity. ***But it was in that process and to that end*** that I edited, removed the bordered box (which trapped space inside of itself), and resized elements according to their importance. I also changed the font from Times New Roman to Boton.

Now be conscious of your eye movement while looking at the slide on the right. Can you feel how your eye slides right down the information? Your brain doesn't worry about missing parts because it knows it caught everything.

In this process of combining appropriate elements into closer proximity to each other, while separating others, you end up with clearer communication.

Proximity is a starting point

All four of these basic principles (contrast, repetition, alignment, and proximity) work together, but proximity is a great place to start. Find the relationships between the elements on the page and group them accordingly. Create space between elements that you want your audience to see as separate elements. From there, be conscious of the other principles—and how they interact between your entire deck of slides—as you build the presentation.

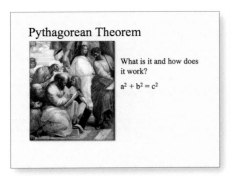

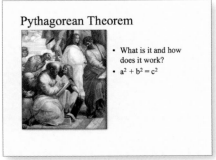

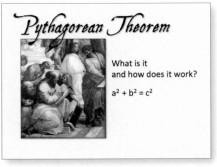

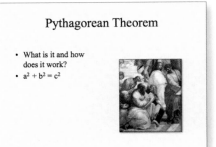

1. The presenter randomly dropped three items on the slide. They have no connection to each other.

2. Let's start with grouping the items together and aligning them. Why not enlarge the beautiful image? Now we have a clear unit of information.

3. Do we really need the bullets in the text? By removing them, we get rid of unnecessary clutter, plus we can move the item closer to the image. A little more space between the paragraphs helps define the two separate thoughts.

4. Instead of using the default font, Times New Roman, find something more visually interesting (and relevant) for the headline. Choose a clean sans serif for the body copy—for clarity, and to prevent a conflict between the two fonts.

Put it all together

These principles act in a *gestalt,* where the whole is more than the sum of its parts. That is, using all these principles *together* is more important and creates a greater effect than using only one principle.

Keep in mind that:

Contrast doesn't mean everything is big—it means there is a contrast *between elements,* and its point is to provide clarity.

Repetition does not mean it all looks the same—it means you have created a *consistent* look that ties your slides together.

Alignment does not mean everything is aligned along *one* line—it means every item on the slide is *visually connected* to some other item, and elements across slides provide a consistent line for visual organization (which translates to an intellectual organization).

Proximity doesn't mean that *everything* is close together— it means items that are closer together create *groups* of information, which in turn provide clarity.

See pages 152–153 for checklists about where to start and what to think about as you pull together your presentation. The following pages show an amazing slide deck from Paul Isakson that incorporates all these principles and provides an exciting and provocative experience.

Name the principles used

This portion of a presentation by Paul Isakson (PaulIsakson.com, posted on his site and used with permission) is a great example of how the conceptual and visual principles outlined in this book do not limit your design, but can liberate your ideas and allow your cohesive thoughts to appear in exciting ways.

Shown on these four pages is the first third of a presentation. Paul firmly believes that one set doesn't fit all—he customizes every presentation to make it relevant for the specific audience and purpose he will be speaking to.

As an exercise in *seeing,* put into words what Paul has done with these slides.

Clarity: What makes the text succinct and clear?

Relevance: What makes the images relevant? The text purposeful?

Animation: Are there places where animation or special transitions might be used effectively?

Plot: Note how he begins and ends his story. Does he involve humanity in the telling of it? Is it organized?

Contrast: Point out contrasts in type, color, size, arrangement, etc.

Repetition: Make a list of the elements that are repeated. Include color, alignments, imagery, fonts, size of fonts, etc.

Alignment: Although there's a lot going on, you'll find very clear alignments throughout the deck. Draw lines to connect them.

Proximity: Note where information is clustered into groups.

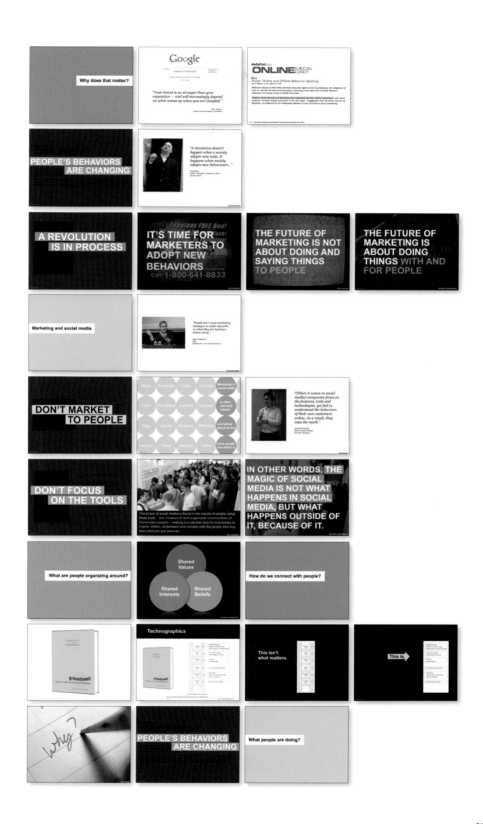

In this segment, you can clearly see the elements that are contrasted, repeated, aligned, and grouped into proximity. Although this format is different from the others in this portion of the full deck, you can see the repetition of colors, fonts, and imagery that unifies these slides with the running theme.

How do these slides tie in with the rest of the deck? Be specific—name names.

Can you see how beautifully he's used the principle of repetition (unity with variety) to tie so many disparate elements together throughout 67 slides?

Note how he brings us full circle—he winds down the piece, lets us know it's ending, ties it together, and says goodbye.

Although this portion of the entire presentation is posted online as a stand-alone product, I'm sure you can imagine how Paul's animated and insightful talk would enhance its message, how the slides actually become an *augmentation* to his wisdom and expertise when given in person.

Great marketers of the future will not be measured by how well they tell stories to their audience, but rather by how well their audience tells stories about them.

Tim Smith

FiNAL THOUGHTS on PRESENTATION Design

BEYOND THE PRINCIPLES

Whoever said, "Don't sweat the small stuff," probably didn't give great presentations. The small stuff—from learning how to set the spacing between paragraphs in your software program to getting the light just right during your talk— can mightily impact your presentation.

Preparation works better than optimism.

John Tollett

Learn your Software

It's not possible to design your slides appropriately if you don't know how to use the software. Yes, you can put the text and the graphics on the slides and move them around, but you need to know how to *control* things to really get the look you want.

There are many books that teach you how to use your chosen application, but there are several features that are so important to the design of your slides that I want to make sure you know them right now.

I can't provide tutorials for all the different software and all the different versions. In this chapter, I provide specific directions for the versions that are current as I write this book: PowerPoint 2007 on the PC, PowerPoint 2008 on a Mac, and Keynote '09 on a Mac. If you're not using one of these, I hope you will be able to find the specific adjustments in your own software, once you know what to look for.

Turn off Autofit

In PowerPoint, one of the most important things to do is **turn off the Autofit feature.** Autofit is what makes your text change size automatically as you type into a text box or resize the box; this feature makes it almost impossible to have a consistent look between your slides—when text is autofit, every slide ends up with differently sized type and different spacing between the lines.

Turn off Autofit in PowerPoint 2007 on a PC or PowerPoint 2008 on a Mac:

1 Select the text box (the *outline* around the text).

2 Right-click* directly on the outline, and choose "Format Shape..." at the bottom of the contextual menu. (If it doesn't say "Format Shape..." at the bottom, the *text box* isn't selected; try again.)

3 In the dialog box that shows up (shown below), click the button that says, "Do not Autofit."

4 Close the dialog box.

On a Mac: If you don't have a two-button mouse, hold down the Control key and click directly on the outline to get the contextual menu.

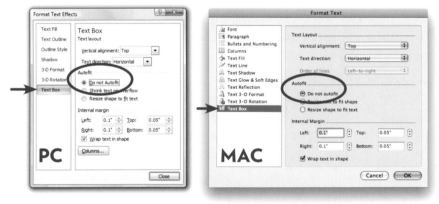

Make sure the "Text Box" option is selected in the left-hand pane.

OR:

On a Mac, to get the dialog box shown above, double-click the edge of a text box, *or* go to the Format menu and choose "Shape...."

On a PC, if you see the little icon (shown right) appear at the bottom-left corner of a text box as you type, click it and choose "Stop Fitting Text to This Placeholder."

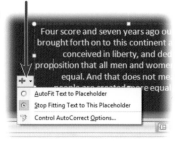

Align text at the top

Text is aligned in text boxes, not only *horizontally* as in a word processor (aligned left, centered, or right), but also *vertically*. This makes the text hug the top of the box, hang in the middle of the box, or sit on the bottom:

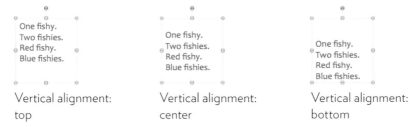

Vertical alignment:
top

Vertical alignment:
center

Vertical alignment:
bottom

When a text box has a default that makes the text align in the *vertical* middle, it becomes almost impossible to align the text boxes across the slides. So you need to know how to recognize the alignment and change it when necessary. Most of the time, for consistency, you want a **top** alignment.

In PowerPoint, to change the vertical alignment, follow Steps 1 and 2 on the opposite page. In those same dialog boxes, toward the top, there are pop-up menus to change the "Vertical alignment."

In Keynote, click in the text box you want to align. Open the Inspector (click the "*i*" icon in the toolbar; *or* from the View menu, choose "Open Inspector"). In the Inspector, click the **T** to display the Text pane. Then click the appropriate icon in the set shown circled, below.

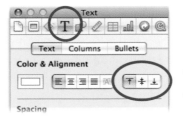

The circled icons are the vertical text alignments.

Adjust the spacing

One thing that makes a huge difference in professionally designed text is **spacing**: spacing between the characters, between the lines, between the paragraphs, and the spacing from the bullet to the text. It is critical that you learn how to control spacing.

Adjust the space between lines

Adding space between lines of text can make it much more readable.

Four score and seven years ago our forefathers brought forth onto this continent a new nation, conceived in liberty, and dedicated to the proposition that all men and women are created equal.

Four score and seven years ago our forefathers brought forth onto this continent a new nation, conceived in liberty, and dedicated to the proposition that all men and women are created equal.

Can you see how a little extra line space makes the text so much easier to read?

In PowerPoint, select the text. Right-click in the text and choose "Paragraph…" from the contextual menu that shows up. (On a Mac with a one-button mouse, Control-click anywhere in the text.)

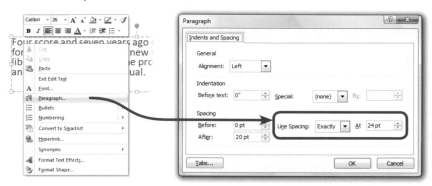

Use the "Line Spacing" options. If you choose "Exactly" (as shown above), you can apply a very specific amount of space: Take the point size of your font, add points to that number to *add* that amount of space between the lines. For instance, if your font size is 18 and you want 6 points of extra space, enter 24 (18 plus 6), as shown above.

In Keynote, open the Inspector and then the Text pane (as explained on the opposite page), and adjust the "Line" slider.

Choose the spacing method from this tiny menu.

Adjust the space between paragraphs

On the computer, a text paragraph is created every time you hit the Return or Enter key. You might think you have three *lines* in, let's say, an address, but your computer sees it as three *paragraphs*. Each bullet point is also considered one paragraph. So to adjust the space between paragraphs, you need to use the *paragraph spacing* "before" and "after," *not* the line-spacing feature.

*Do not **ever** hit the Enter or Return key twice to make space between the paragraphs!* That creates an unsightly and unnecessarily huge gap.

One little fishy went to market.
Two little fishies stayed home.
One little fishy ate bean soup.
The blue little fishies ate none.

One little fishy went to market.

Two little fishies stayed home.

One little fishy ate bean soup.

The blue little fishies ate none.

If you adjust the **line spacing,** *all* the lines will have more space between them.

If you adjust the **paragraph spacing,** the *lines* stay together and space is added either above (before) or below (after) the *paragraph.*

In PowerPoint, select *all the paragraphs* to which you want to apply spacing. Right-click in the text and choose "Paragraph…." (or Control-click if you have a one-button mouse on a Mac). Use the Spacing "Before" and "After."

Paragraph space *before* adds space *above* the **selected** paragraph. You might want to use this to separate body copy from the preceding headline.

Paragraph space *after* adds space *below* the selected paragraph. Select and separate all the bullet points this way.

In Keynote:

1 Select *all the paragraphs* in the text box to which you want to apply paragraph spacing.

2 Open the Inspector (from the View menu, choose "Open Inspector"), and click the **T** to see the Text pane.

3 Drag the "Before Paragraph" *or* "After Paragraph" sliders, or enter a number in the field.

121

Adjust the space from the bullet to the text

You probably think this is a bit fussy, but once you start really *seeing* type on the slide, you'll start noticing the space between the bullets and the text. Different applications usually set the bullet too far away or too close, but you can adjust it.

• One little fishy went to market.	• One little fishy went to market.
• Two little fishies stayed home.	• Two little fishies stayed home.
• One little fishy ate bean soup.	• One little fishy ate bean soup.
• The blue little fishies ate none.	• The blue little fishies ate none.

The bullets in the left-hand example are too far away from the text; they're not in proximity to each other. On the right, each bullet has a relationship with its text.

In PowerPoint, you might think that to adjust the spacing between the bullets and the text, you would use the "Bullets and Numbering" pane. Wrong. You need the "Paragraph" pane, as shown below. *Select the text you want to format,* then right-click (or Control-click on a Mac) and choose "Paragraph...."

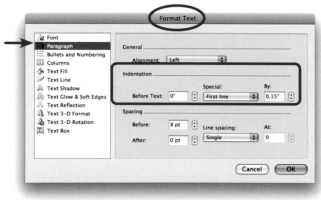

If your bullets are one-liners, as above:

1 In the "Before Text" field, enter 0 (zero).

2 From the "Special" menu, choose "First line."

3 In the "By" field, enter a small amount to scoot the text just a wee bit to the right of the bullet.

In Keynote:

1 Select the text you want to format.

2 Open the Inspector and click the **T**.

3 Click the "Bullets" tab.

4 Select a bullet type from the menu.

5 In the "Text Indent" field, click the up arrow until you see the first line of text move to the right as much as you need. The larger the type, the higher this number needs to be.

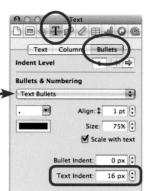

Hang the bullets; align the text

This is really important. When your bullet points have more than one line of text, the text needs to align to the other lines of text. That is, the text should *not* wrap back under the bullet; the bullet should "hang" out to the left.

• One little fishy went to market.
• Two little fishies stayed home.
• One little fishy ate bean soup.
• The blue little fishies ate none.

• One little fishy went to market.
• Two little fishies stayed home.
• One little fishy ate bean soup.
• The blue little fishies ate none.

On the left, do you see how messy the text appears when it wraps back under the bullet? On the right, the bullet points are so neat and tidy.

In PowerPoint, select the text you want to format, then right-click and choose "Paragraph…" (or on a Mac, Control-click in the selected text).

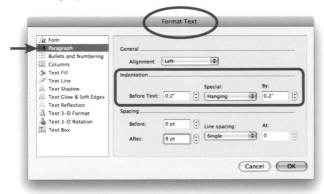

To "hang" the bullets:

1 From the "Special" menu, choose "Hanging."

2 In the "By" field, enter a small amount to scoot the text a wee bit to the right of the bullet.

3 *Enter the same amount* in the "Before Text" field.

In Keynote, follow the directions on the opposite page (bottom of the page) to open the Text pane. As you continuously click the up arrow in the "Text Indent" field, you'll see the *second* line of text move to the right, and when the second line gets lined up with the first line, *both lines* will move together to the right, beautifully aligned.

Don't squish the images

In PowerPoint it's easy to resize an image in the wrong way and squish it out of proportion. There's a simple rule to follow: Resize an image using a corner handle, *not* any handle on the edges.

If you grab any of the handles on the *edges* and drag, you'll squish the image.

To tilt an image, use this handle.

Grab any *corner* handle and drag, and the image will resize in proportion (in the proper "aspect ratio").

photo by Laura Egley Taylor

In Keynote, the default is set so it's not possible to resize the image out of proportion, no matter which handle you drag.

If you *do* want to change the proportions, open the Inspector and use the Metrics pane (the ruler icon). Uncheck the box to "Constrain proportions." Now you can either enter a specific size, or drag any handle on the image. (To constrain proportions while that box is unchecked, hold down the Shift key when resizing.)

To tilt an image, hold down the Command key and drag a corner.

Handouts

Handouts are a critical part of most presentations. There are times when it's not necessary to provide a handout—perhaps you are giving a keynote address and it's more like a speech with visuals, or you're delivering a philosophical commentary with lots of discussion.

But most often, your audience wants something tangible they can take back to the office or home. Handouts make it easier for attendees to follow along, to take notes, and to get an idea of when your presentation will end.

If you have charts or tables of data, create a handout so everyone can actually read the charts and make notes on them.

If you provide directions on how to do something, make a handout (we humans can rarely write down directions correctly while hearing them in a talk).

If you have contact information, resources, or web addresses, make a handout—never expect people to write down a complex web address correctly.

Visually, make your handout connect with your slide presentation so your audience remembers who you are. That is, pull in the same colors and fonts that they saw on the screen. And you can put your logo on the handout; it's the perfect and preferred place for it.

The truth about handouts

You may have heard this rule: "NEVER provide handouts because it will distract listeners from your talk as they try to read ahead on the handout and listen to you at the same time."

Balderdash.

Trust me, I can find plenty to distract myself with besides your handout. I've got my cell phone with access to the Internet and email and Twitter. I've got my laptop with access to the work that I'm behind on. I've got a notepad and pen—you might think I'm busily scribbling notes, but I'm actually sketching an outline for a novel. And I've got the coffee cart down the hall and no one's going to stop me from walking out and getting a cup. So don't flatter yourself that your *handout* will distract me from your talk.

Quite the contrary. Your thoughtfully created handout tells me you respect me enough to have created it for me, and that in turn makes me pay a little more attention.

As an attendee, I WANT to take notes. I want to circle key points on your handout and make notes to myself about what to check up on, what to report back with, what to add to my own report, etc. I want to write down interesting things you say. Taking notes while someone is talking is a skill we learned long ago—that's how we got through school. And if your handouts are created thoughtfully, the attendees can follow along with you on the handout, only making notes where necessary for their own enlightenment.

To design your handout, use the same principles of design you read about in Chapters 7 through 10 on contrast, repetition, alignment, and proximity.

Handouts can be very simple (merely an outline to follow along), or a list of highlights and resources, or they might be complex and useful enough for other instructors to use as teaching materials.

It's a permanent record

What your audience sees on the overhead screen is temporary, and there is no guarantee they will remember it correctly; what you give them to take back to the office is permanent.

Your presentation software, of course, lets you print your slides in a variety of ways—with notes, without notes, notes only, slides only, etc. This can be handy, but not particularly effective. For instance, if you've expanded the number of slides so you can present each item clearly, you might have so many slides that each handout would be twenty or thirty pages. And if you've created your presentation to *augment* your speaking points instead of putting your entire talk on the slides, the slides alone won't mean much to someone else.

So that means it's an extra load of work to create a useful piece to leave behind. But if you create something valuable, it increases the effectiveness and impact of your entire presentation. Your attendees will appreciate it and you will look like a professional. They will have something that reminds them of you, and the influence of your presentation will last much longer.

Remember on page 47 where I encouraged you to let go of putting your logo on every slide? The slides are transitory, but your logo and other branding elements on a nicely designed handout is much more valuable (see page 139).

Very often, you will be giving the same presentation more than once, so the work you do on the handout will be amortized over the number of presentations. Plus if you put that much trouble into a presentation, you're more likely to *want* to do it again! And each time it gets better.

If you have maps or charts that you want people to actually read (or even see), put them in a handout.

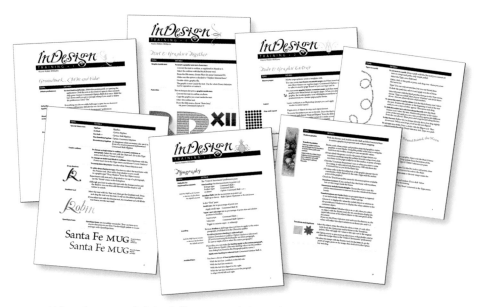

When I present Adobe InDesign workshops, I cannot expect attendees to remember everything I say. I have a moral obligation to leave behind something useful.

Post your speaker notes

When you post presentations online at sites like PowerShow.com and SlideShare.net, you can include your speaker notes. Unfortunately, most people, instead of providing speaker notes, simply post the slide information in text format so there's no extra data besides what's on the slide.

Remember, the point of the speaker notes is to provide me, the viewer, with further insights that elaborate on your amazing presentation! And by putting these insights into the speaker notes, you don't have to put everything you know on those tiny slides.

Ignore these Rules

You have certainly heard or read a number of rules for creating digital presentations. And I've provided a number of guidelines throughout this book. But the variety of presentations is so broad and multifaceted that I must take issue with some of the really strong pronouncements I have heard and read. Some of these pronouncements might be grounded in good information, but have been misinterpreted by non-designers who have to create slideshows and are unsure of themselves and so take things a bit too literally.

When considering which guidelines to follow for your specific talk and the presentation design, you must always be mindful of to whom you are speaking and in what kind of facility. Are you speaking in a boardroom or a ballroom or a gymnasium? At a scholarly conference or a teen workshop or a suicide-prevention center? To actors or scientists?

Guidelines are great; they give you a terrific place to start. But many rules are made to be broken. Let's look closely at the rules you may have heard proclaimed with authority.

Never read a slide aloud

Baloney.

You have surely heard a hundred times, "Don't read your slides!" And this gets misinterpreted to mean that one should never read what is on the slide. I have actually seen presenters start to read aloud the few words on the slide and then stop, muttering, "Oh, I shouldn't read it."

The point is not about reading your slides. The point is to avoid putting your talk on the slides. *Don't put your talk on the slides and you won't have to read it.*

I *always* read my slides aloud. For one thing, I don't have much text on the slide and that text is what I'm talking about, so as I begin to talk about that point, it just happens to be (duh) what's on the slide. Thus the attendees get the information in two ways—they see it and they hear it. And they have it on their handout.

Secondly, I never assume that the people sitting in the back can actually read the slide, and even people sitting more forward might not have great eyesight, if any at all. So when I have a slide like the one below, showing a Shakespearean quote that I'm going to talk about, I want to make sure everyone knows the quote. Because it has been so hammered into everyone's heads that one should "Never read the slides!," I sometimes preface it with something like, "I'm going to read this quote in case those of you in the back can't see it clearly."

I also make sure that my laptop is positioned between me and the audience so when I read the slide from my computer, I am looking at the audience members, not at the screen with my back to them.

If you have words on a slide and never say those words, you run the risk that your audience gets confused about the relationship between what you are saying and what they are seeing.

The real problem

As I've mentioned before, the admonition to not read your slides actually refers to a different problem—that you have put all of your information onto the slide and are using that as if you're reading a paper. The problem is not really that you are reading the slide—*the problem is that you have put everything you're going to say on that slide.* Don't do that.

PowerPoint Slides	PowerPoint Slides
• Highlight key points or reinforce what the facilitator is talking about	• Highlight or reinforce
• Should be short and to the point, including only key words and phrases for visuals and reinforcement	• Short statements, key words and phrases
• In order for your presentation to fit on most screens, text and images should be placed within 95 percent of the PowerPoint slide. This "action safe" area is shown on the next slide.	• Action-safe area

With all your text on the slide, you have no choice but to read it.

Pick out the key points and put those on the slide. Fill out the slide with your talk.

Never use serif typefaces

Hogwash.

Feel free to use lovely serif typefaces *if you set them large enough to be read.* It's true that on a computer screen, many sans serif faces (not all) can be easier to read because the strokes tend to be thicker and the letterforms are simpler and they don't have small parts that can get lost in the pixels of the monitor. This is especially true of sans serifs that have been designed specifically for the screen.

But if the type can be set large enough, use a serif face if you like. It creates a completely different look and feel (usually a little warmer) than does a no-nonsense sans serif, so take advantage of that.

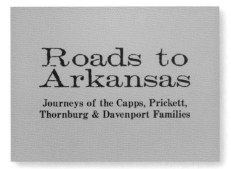

There's a wide range of serif fonts. Don't be afraid of using one, as long as it's large enough and bold enough. Do avoid fonts with very thin strokes, such as Didot, unless you can set it really large:

Didot

This font is the classic Garamond, eminently readable, even on a screen (when set large enough).

Baby goes on a spree.

Never use animation

Pish tosh.

Since you've read this book, you already know that animation can be an extremely useful tool for clarifying important points, calling attention to items, or creating transitions to new subtopics, etc.

What this rule really means is, "Never use the kind of animation that's going to make your audience hate you." That is, don't type every word onto the page. Don't swirl everything in from the side. Don't use corny little animated images. Don't use a checkerboard transition between *every* slide. I know it's irresistible, but we're all moving on into this new millennium and looking for clarity in our presentations. Use animation when it can enhance clarity.

This is part of Dave Rohr's "Roads to Arkansas" presentation. As he talks about the migration of the family, the arrows appear and move toward the destinations, calling attention to themselves and making the path clear.

Never use more than one background

Fiddle dee dee.

As you have seen throughout this book, there are good reasons to use different backgrounds. You just have to make sure that you know *why* and can put into words *why* you are changing the background. A reason such as, "I'm tired of the blue spaceship background and now I want a green forest" is not a good reason.

When the background changes during your presentation, it sends a signal to the audience. Make sure this is the signal you want to send—a new topic, a change in thought, a special callout. Remember, all those busy minds in your audience are going to start processing information about the background as soon as it changes, especially if it's an interesting background. If the background doesn't complement what you're talking about, you're going to lose your audience for a little bit as they work that out in their heads.

So use more than one background *when it's relevant and provides clarity.*

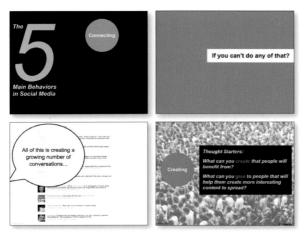

These slides are from Paul Isakson's deck that I showed you on pages 110–113. Although there are different backgrounds, can you see elements that tie them together? Be sure to take a look at all the slides in his example to see how well he uses different backgrounds as repetitive themes.

Never make a slide without a graphic on it

Tilly fally.

A nice typographic treatment of your text is perfectly acceptable and welcome. If your slide is strictly type, just make sure it's clear—is the typeface legible, is it large enough, is the color of the type a good contrast with the background, is there contrast on the page that makes me want to look at it?

If your content is boring and your type is boring, some random graphic is not going to make it better. If you're using a default template with small black type on a large white background, indiscriminate clip art in the corners is not going to fix it.

Of course, use relevant graphics and even animated ones *when the image clarifies your point.*

Seriously, do these arbitrary graphics add anything to this presentation opening?

Above, we have nice text on a template background, perfectly sufficient. Below is a slide with simply text. It looks much more sophisticated without haphazard images.

Never use more than five bullet points per slide

Bibble babble.

One problem with this rule is that it makes people think it's okay to put five bullet points on every slide. The more important thing to remember is that *you don't need to put all your bullet points on one slide in the first place,* as I explained in Chapter 3. Once you understand that concept and start spreading out your slides, deciding what needs to be expanded into multiple slides, and determining which collections of bullet points need to stay on one slide, you'll find the right number—based on the needs of your presentation, not on an arbitrary number.

You might need six points or even seven (most often you'll need fewer)—*just make sure you can put into words* why you *must* have them all on one slide (and make sure they're big enough to read). If your reasoning creates clarity in your presentation, then use bullet points with glee.

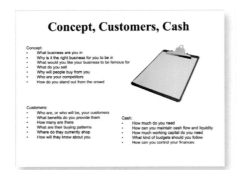

This slide has more than five bullet points on it, but that's not the main problem or the only problem, is it?

To create an opening for our story, let's add contrast with a bold font and move those lists onto separate slides. The client loves his clipboard and uses it on everything, so we'll let it stay.

Depending on how this talk is structured, these slides might be used to provide introductions to individual sections, which then move into one slide per bullet point.

Never use more than two or three words per bullet point

Flapdoodle.

This rule goes along with, "Never use more than six words on a slide." It's just not possible to lay down a rule like this and expect it to be followed, and there are many many many incredibly amazing slide presentations that break this rule.

Make every word count, be as succinct as possible, but don't *arbitrarily* limit the number of words because of this rule. Be clear.

These two slides are also from Paul Isakson's deck. He's got no problem using a dozen words on these slides. Can you read it? Is the message clear? Can you imagine Paul expounding on these thoughts?

Also consider how someone else might have set both these ideas as bullet points on one slide (small, black Arial on a white background). I'm sure you can see the greater impact that results from separating the points and expanding onto more slides.

Never use PowerPoint

Hooey.

As I mentioned in the introduction, if you're giving a speech or certain type of lecture, you probably don't need multimedia. But if you're giving a *presentation,* then people expect some sort of visuals.

PowerPoint is not the problem—a *presenter's* ineffective use of PowerPoint is the problem. Anyone who decrees that no one should ever use PowerPoint is someone who hasn't learned how to use the tool properly himself. So the message to you is really, "Learn to use your software and learn to create an effective presentation."

Never turn the lights off. Never turn the lights on.

Moonshine.

Once again, these mantras get repeated without a real understanding of the intention. It's true that you don't want to be a disembodied voice speaking through the blackness, but neither do you want the slides that you worked so hard on to be washed out and difficult to read because all the lights are on (or worse, the lights are pointed right at the screen).

Ideally, you'd like dim lights in the audience (but enough light so they can take notes and so you can see them and their reactions to you), some light on you standing next to the screen, and the screen itself with as little light as possible. Newer auditoriums and boardrooms are fitted for this kind of scenario, with many combinations of lighting possibilities.

If you're going to stand in total brightness and your slides will be illegible, then why bring a slide presentation? Just give a speech. If you know the room is either all dark or all light, bring your own lamp to place near you.

The important thing to remember is that lighting *is* an issue, so be aware and, if possible, check out your situation beforehand on the chance that you can do something about it.

Never provide handouts before your talk

Piffle.

But you already know this is piffle because you read Chapter 13 about the importance of handouts and the importance of giving them to your audience before you speak. And remember, go ahead and brand your handouts with your logo!

Never use pie charts

Balderdash.

One can't make a blanket statement that all pie charts are wrong. Pie charts are not the problem—a *presenter's* ineffective use of pie charts is the problem.

Use a pie chart when it is the best way to present your information clearly. Remember, the percentage numbers in a pie chart must *add up to* 100 percent. And if there are too many pieces in the pie, it becomes ineffective because you can't see the differences between the slices clearly. But if your data can show me the relative size of one thing versus a couple of other things, then a simple pie chart can be efficient and clear. And it's fun to make a slice pull out of the pie and call attention to itself (as long as it clarifies the information!).

Never use Arial or Helvetica

True.

I'm sorry, but this is true. If you are a brilliant and trained designer, you can use Arial or Helvetica in ways that aren't dreadfully dull. But for most people, if you plop together your presentation with the default Arial that appears on your PowerPoint page, you are doomed to mediocrity.

If you insist on using Arial or Helvetica, buy the entire professional Helvetica font family instead of using what is built into your machine. Only if you buy the whole family can you get the heavy bolds and thin thins that don't have the patina of boring all over them.

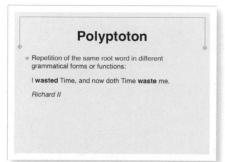

This is the default Arial/Helvetica.

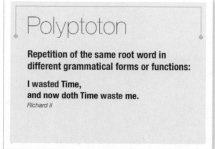

With a little work and a financial investment in the professional font family, you can make Helvetica look less tired and worn out.

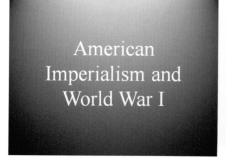

Times or Times New Roman has the same problem. It's a skillfully designed typeface, but now has the look of an old default workhorse that needs a break.

Even if you haven't bought any new fonts, you have a good collection on your computer. Try some others (above is Rockwell).

Listen to your Eyes

The most important skill you can learn in design is to **see**. This chapter is a quiz designed to help you learn to see the various principles I've outlined in this book.

Do the slides on these pages seem a little small? Remember, if you're in the back of a large room or if the screen is fairly small, the slides might seem about this big in person. Keep that in mind as you design.

And don't forget, as you go through these examples, that a large part of slide design is determining what gets to stay on the slide and what goes somewhere else—to another slide, the speaker notes, the handout, or maybe to the trash.

> . . . for in such business
> Action is eloquence,
>   and the eyes of the ignorant
> More learnèd than the ears.
>
> Volumnia in *Coriolanus*, 3.2.78–80

Quiz: Listen to your eyes

We learn best if we can put into words what the problem is and what the solution might be. So as you go through these slides, spend a few minutes trying to say the problems and solutions out loud.

CLARITY: Choose the slide in each set whose text is most clear.

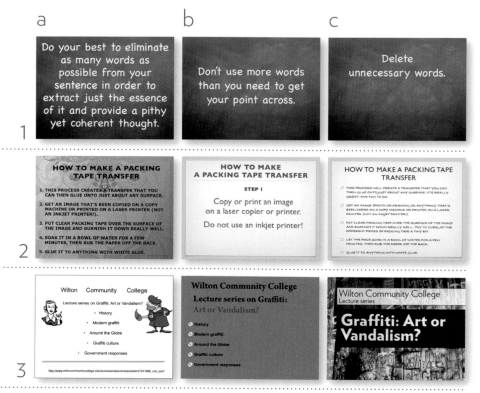

Remember, part of the principle of clarity is making sure there's nothing useless or distracting on the slide. Does *everything* have to go on one slide? What exactly muddles the message on some of these? Can you name the steps it might take to get to a clean, professional look?

1 ....

....

2 ....

....

3 ....

....

RELEVANCE: Choose the set of slides whose background or imagery does NOT confuse the communication because it is relevant to the topic.

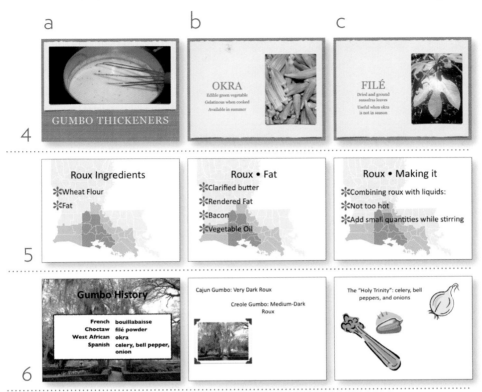

Exactly what is it that makes some of the imagery not relevant?

4

5

6

ANIMATION: In each set of slides, describe what kind of animation, transitions, video, or audio clips could be used to enhance the communication.

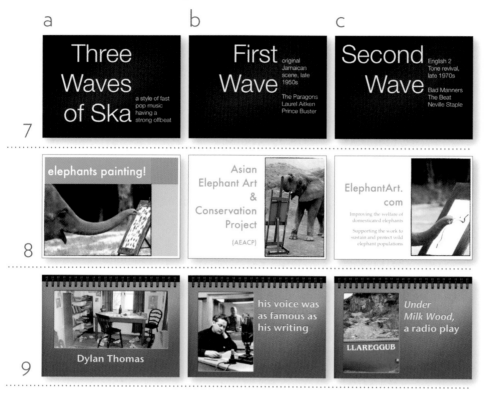

Why would you *not* want the text on all the slides to animate onto the slide?

7 ....

....

....

8 ....

....

....

9 ....

....

....

PLOT: Choose the best slide in each set with which to *begin* the presentation.

a   b   c

10

11

Why are the other slides not the best as openers?

10 ....

11 ....

PLOT: Choose the best slide in each set with which to *end* the presentation.

12

13

Why are the other slides not the best as final slides?

12 ....

13 ....

CONTRAST: Choose the set of slides that your eyes are drawn to because of the contrast.

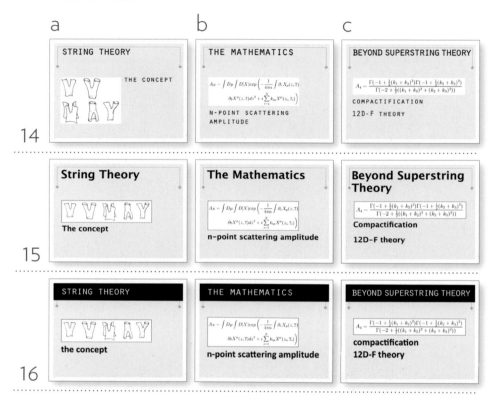

How does the contrast help to clarify the communication? Does it change your impression of the information in any way?

16 ....

....

....

17 ....

....

....

18 ....

....

....

REPETITION: Choose the slide set that is most unified by repetitive elements in the design.

Name the repetitive elements in the set you chose.
Are there other repetitive elements you could use on the other slides to create more unified and coherent looks?

19
....
....
....

20
....
....
....

21
....
....
....

ALIGNMENT: Choose the slide set whose alignments help to clarify the information and make it easier to comprehend.

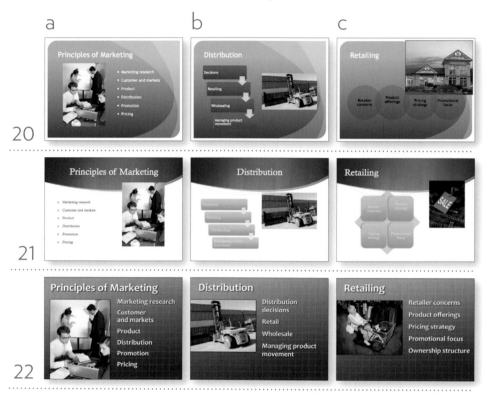

Draw lines on all the slides so you can clearly see where alignments are happening—or not.

22

23

24

PROXIMITY: Which slide set presents the information with clarity and cohesiveness through a good use of proximity?

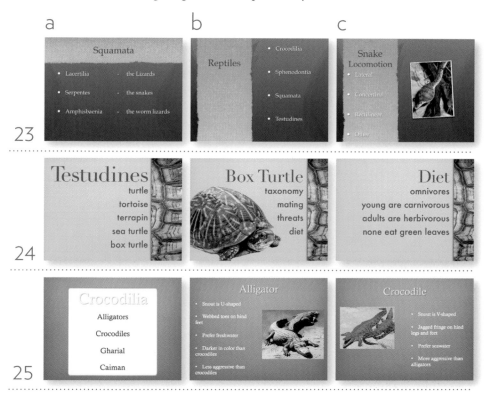

Can you put into words exactly what each of the other slides needs to improve its communication through proximity?

25 ....

....

....

26 ....

....

....

27 ....

....

....

HANDOUTS: The slide set below has too much text. Make a list of how you could change it. Decide a) what text or image stays on each slide, b) what can be expanded onto more slides, c) what text is in your talk/speaker notes, and d) what text or image is in your handout.

26

Suggestions will vary, of course.

26a
....

....

  b
....

....

....

  c
....

....

....

  d
....

....

....

OVERALL: Critique this deck of slides. Consider how (in person) some elements might enter individually as you talk about them, and consider what kinds of transitions might be used. Write down what seems to work well, and what might be improved. Use the terms you learned in this book and the checklists on the two following pages. Be specific.

27

 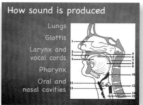 

These slides use a dissolve transition so all that *appears* to change is the gold text.

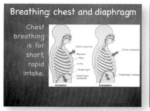 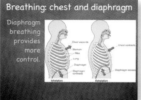 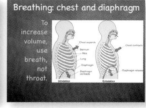

The green answers slide in after the question is asked.

  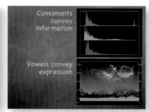

What works and what might be improved?

27

....

....

....

....

....

....

....

....

....

Checklist for info

○ Learn how to use your software.

○ Develop your text and organizational structure before you put it on the slides.

○ Edit your text so it is clear and relevant.

○ Decide which points should stay on one slide and which ones you can spread out to other slides.

○ Gather up a few graphics, if you plan to use them. You will probably think of others you need as you go along.

○ Consider where you might use animation, video, or sound clips to add interest and to illuminate your information.

○ Choose a relevant background, a relevant template, or design a relevant look. You will refine it as you go along, but at least get the basic structure in place.

○ Create an opening slide.

○ Create an overview slide, if relevant (you might create several of these in your deck, as you move from topic to topic).

○ Start laying in the slides until you've pretty much got your look going and your outline on the slides you need.

○ Start refining the design of the slides according to the basic principles of contrast, repetition, alignment, and proximity.

○ Be sure to create a winding down and ending to your tale of information.

Checklist for slides

○ Are your talking points edited down to the most important elements?

○ Are all slides clean and uncrowded (because you created as many slides as you needed)?

○ Did you avoid putting your entire talk as text on the slides? (If you don't put your talk on your slides, you won't end up reading the slides.)

○ Did you eliminate any unecessary bullets? Please don't ever use dashes instead of bullets—they're so unpleasant to look at.

○ Is everything on your slide relevant and necessary?

○ Is animation, audio, and video used only to clarify and to call attention to relevant items?

○ Do you have a beginning, a middle, and an end? Is it clear to your audience when you have reached the end?

○ Is there enough contrast on the slides to draw people's eyes toward them? Does the contrast help clarify the information?

○ Are there repetitive elements throughout the deck that visually tie it all together?

○ Is every item on every slide visually connected to something else on the slide? Are there alignments across your entire deck that help to keep it visually organized?

○ Are your bullets (if you're using them) close enough (but not too close) to the bullet copy so they appear like they belong together?

○ Are items that are intellectually connected also visually connected by being closer together? Are all your groups of info related to each other?

○ Did you create a useful handout that attendees will want to keep?

○ If you're posting your entire presentation online, are you including your speaker notes as well?

Sources for
fonts/images/video/sound

Professional images, video, etc:

iStockphoto.com
(see the coupon on page 159)

Veer.com

Shutterstock.com

Free images and more :

Commons.WikiMedia.org

www.MorgueFile.com

www.DreamsTime.com

Fonts:

MyFonts.com

Veer.com

FontShop.com

FontBureau.com

There are thousands of low-quality (but sometimes quite useful) free fonts online. Search for "free fonts"

iStockphoto.com images used:

sale tag: wragg 10511326

forklift: lagereek 3346468

turtle background: ntripp 8340053

passports: kirza 1648185

graffiti: DaiPhoto 2532985

business meeting: endopack 3138945

go-cart shopper: imageegami 10379737

elephants painting:

    polispoliviou 7184553

    Vicky_bennett 382294

    Hirkophoto 4887474

game letter cubes: 408326

game pieces: magnet creative 4190979

game, man playing: Photodjo 9267387

game, girl playing: lisafx 659308

renaissance paper: Wadders 330118

Index

Rediscover your passion *for creativity*

WATCH
READ
CREATE

Unlimited online access to all Peachpit, Adobe Press, Apple Training and New Riders videos and books, as well as content from other leading publishers including: O'Reilly Media, Focal Press, Sams, Que, Total Training, John Wiley & Sons, Course Technology PTR, Class on Demand, VTC and more.

No time commitment or contract required!
Sign up for one month or a year.
All for $19.99 a month

SIGN UP TODAY
peachpit.com/creativeedge

creative
edge